RAILWAYS THROUG
AIREDALE & WHAR

Martin Bairstow

Published by Martin Bairstow, 41 Galloway Lane, Pudsey, West Yorkshire
Printed by Allanwood Press Ltd., Stanningley, Pudsey

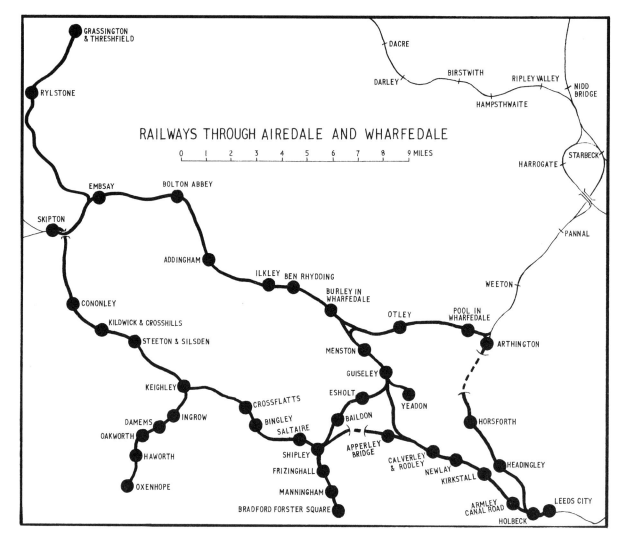

RAILWAYS THROUGH AIREDALE AND WHARFEDALE

0 1 2 3 4 5 6 7 8 9 MILES

Introduction
Travelling under the Axe

The lines featured in this book are those upon which I first became acquainted with the art of rail travel. My local station was Apperley Bridge and from the Spring of 1963 I was old enough to make journeys on my own. From September 1963, when I started at Bradford Grammar School, until March 1965, when both stations closed, I commuted between Apperley Bridge and Frizinghall. Throughout this period one journeyed under constant threat that the axe would soon fall.

In order to service about 75 passengers each week-day, Apperley Bridge boasted a station master, two clerks, two leading porters, a junior porter to clean the signal box windows etc, a vanman who distributed one van load of parcels each day around Rawdon and Yeadon and a goods checker who ensured that the odd wagon of coal in the goods yard had the right labels on.

My house was about one mile from the station and each morning I set off at the last minute and sprinted to catch the 8.25 train. One day I tripped and fell and needed the attention of the station first aid box. I don't suppose

that facility is available nowadays at stations manned only by a saver strip machine.

There were generally a few passengers about as I purchased my half return to Frizinghall for 7d but the main activity on the station was the listing on sheets of paper of the parcels which had arrived by train and were to be delivered by the van driver. The final column on these sheets was headed 'received in good order by' and the van driver used to invent the signatures of the recipients as he deposited each successive package in the doorway or coal house. Most of the parcels were mail order goods and most of the customers were out at work though it made little difference if they were in.

The train was a twin car Derby built dmu with only one car powered which was adequate for this route. Only on Summer Saturdays was it loaded up to eight cars because it then worked a Bradford Forster Square to Scarborough service. In all the 18 months, a train was never cancelled and I was late for school only once. There were plenty of minor delays, however, usually caused by time spent unloading parcels at Apperley Bridge and Shipley.

The quadruple track route was busy with both passenger and freight. My train was the 8.05 from Leeds which travelled on the 'fast' line and was overtaken just before reaching Apperley Bridge by the 8.10 dmu to Skipton, first stop Bingley. At least twice, this train was stopped at Apperley Bridge by the signalman, on instructions from control, to pick up one or two passengers for Keighley who would otherwise have been delayed by as much as 25 minutes through the 7.40 Leeds – Bradford running too late to catch its Skipton connection at Shipley. That was service.

Our arrival at Frizinghall was a couple of minutes before the 8.30 Bradford Forster Square – Morecambe called in the other direction. This was often 'Britannia' hauled but sometimes a 'Peak' class diesel. One morning I and a dozen other passengers used this train to get back from Manningham when our driver forgot to stop at Frizinghall. That is one of very few occasions that I have known trains miss booked stops. Frizinghall station had seen better days. The former buildings on the road bridge had been demolished and the booking office relocated in what had been a waiting room on the up platform. After September 1963, its last train was at 7.41 pm in order to save staffing costs although there were plenty of trains passing through after that hour. This type of false economy applied at quite a number of stations so that in the evening and on Sundays 'local' trains ran virtually non stop. This practice tended to die out later as one of the benefits of introducing unstaffed stations.

My grandparents moved to Ilkley in April 1964. Taking advantage of their new location in a rail served town, I lost little time in arranging a visit. From Apperley Bridge there were two ways of reaching Ilkley. The problem of going via Shipley was that, outside peak hours, the hourly interval trains gave about a ¾ hour wait in both directions. The alternative was to travel one station towards Leeds and change there. This possibility was usually thwarted by Ilkley trains not stopping at Calverley & Rodley but a Saturday afternoon visit was possible by this route.

In those days 'ordinary' single and return tickets could be purchased to any station on BR at 3d per mile provided that three days notice was given in the event of no fare for that destination having been calculated since the previous fares increase. But for selected local journeys 'cheap single' and 'day return' tickets were available often at less than half the 'ordinary' fare. I was sufficiently conversant with the arrangements to know that I would have to book separate day returns for the two sections of my journey.

One of the clerks was on duty in the booking office as I entered the station from the road bridge. The first preliminary towards obtaining a ticket was to knock on the booking office window in order that the person within might drop what he was doing, raise the hatch and begin to sell rail travel.

A half return to Calverley & Rodley please
What do you want to go there for?
I need to change there for Ilkley
Why don't you go via Shipley?
Because there isn't a connection
Well you'll have to book single both ways
But I want a return
It won't cost you any more

But I may not be able to get a ticket at Calverley & Rodley on the way back (and if there's one thing to which I object it is handing over excess fares at the end of a journey without any receipt being issued. In those days tickets were never sold on the train)
If I sell you a return I will have to cut a ticket in half
I'm sorry but I want a return ticket.

I stood my ground and duly exchanged 4d for an Edmondson card ticket cut diagonally in half. The clerk's grievance was that a printed child ticket was in issue for single but not return journeys to Calverley & Rodley.

It only remained to descend the 42 steps to reach the platform and join a two car dmu for the four minute journey which compared very favourably with the time required to buy the ticket.

Nobody joined the train at Calverley & Rodley and I was the only one to alight. I stepped onto the platform adjacent to where the station staff was standing. He enquired: 'Is this where you want to be? Carvley?' (the first l is not pronounced). I assured him that it was, whereupon he invited the guard to proceed to the next parish. He then followed me up the staircase towards the ticket office.

A half return to Ilkley please

Without question an Edmondson card ticket (a complete one this time) was put through the date stamp in exchange for 1s6d, a sum I cheerfully disbursed doubtless in anticipation of a grandparental grant. It was only on the staircase back to the platform that I noticed that the ticket bore the previous day's date. So once again I disturbed the man's peace by knocking on the booking office window to point out this defect in my travel document. He said he didn't think anyone would notice but he would alter the machine in case there were any more customers. I took the opportunity of confirming that my train would be on platform 3, the down slow line, since Ilkley trains could use either of the pairs of tracks between Leeds and Apperley Junction.

The journey to Ilkley was accomplished in one of the 300 hp Derby built units which were introduced on this line in 1959 and are still in operation. In those days they were painted in lined green but the chevrons at each end had given way to yellow warning panels. The front compartment in the trailer was reserved for first class passengers but ordinary mortals could enjoy a front end view when the power car was leading.

In 1964, the view beyond the immediate lineside was much as it is today but the narrower view through the front cab of that dmu was of a scene virtually unchanged from Midland Railway days. At least all the facilities were there even though some were a little decayed or falling into disuse. Stored in sidings at Apperley Junction and Calverley & Rodley, were sets of excursion coaches. These were a familiar sight at a number of locations before somebody decided that it was 'uneconomic' to keep rolling stock for occasional use only.

The track was quadruple between Leeds and Shipley whilst the Ilkley line was double throughout including the extension to Skipton and the route through Otley which still made its junctions at Menston and Burley. The Yeadon branch still trailed in at Rawdon Junction. Every station and junction had a signal box with a forest of semaphore signals.

The stations nearly all had gas lighting of the 'modern' type which had pilot lights. As a sign of neglect, only those nearest the buildings were serviceable at most stations. It has become too much trouble to replace mantles at the extreme ends of the platforms. On the lines covered by this book, only Bradford Forster Square had fluorescent lights. Keighley and Armley Canal Road managed electric light bulbs but Arthington, Bolton Abbey and Embsay were still illuminated by oil lamps.

At each intermediate station, the arrival of the dmu was attended by a porter. Those with strong vocal chords shouted the name of the station. Other duties included closing the doors and collecting the tickets which at the end of the week had to be sorted into numerical order for every type and originating station and sent to an office in Newcastle. At Guiseley and Ilkley a platform barrow would be on hand for any parcels which might arrive on the train for delivery by road vehicle on Monday morning. Each goods yard still contained the odd wagon of coal.

On the return journey we hit Calverley & Rodley at the rush hour when within the space of two minutes there were three trains booked to call and on this day all three were there at once. As I alighted from the Ilkley – Leeds on platform 2, a Leeds – Skipton via Ilkley service was drawing into platform 3 (the other side of the centre island) but my sights were directed at the Leeds – Bradford local which was already standing at platform 1. The same leading porter was in attendance. On learning that I desired the Bradford train and pausing only to catch the attention of the driver of the Ilkley – Leeds, he escorted me across the track in front of it but to no avail. He assured me that there would be another one soon and proceeded up the staircase to his office.

A few minutes later he returned:

Did you just get off that train over there?
Yes
Where have you come from?
Ilkley
Where are you going?
Apperley Bridge
But what are you doing here?
Changing trains
And did you come here this dinner time?
Yes
Where were you going then?
From Apperley Bridge to Ilkley
And where are you going now?
From Ilkley to Apperley Bridge
Why didn't you go via Shipley?
Because there wasn't a connection.

He reaffirmed that I wouldn't have to wait long and went about his business again.

I recall once sitting on my bicycle outside Calverley & Rodley station when I observed the incumbent emerge from his booking office and throw his tealeaves out into the street. This was an unpleasant habit but how it summed up the gulf between the two worlds on either side of that station entrance. Just as that railman didn't care where the contents of his teapot landed once they had left railway property, so the public outside neither knew nor cared what travel facilities were available within that sanctum. With more than 50 departures each weekday, one could connect with services to any part of the BR system or beyond. But if you had tried to do so they would not have known what you were talking about.

The days when residents of Calverley would walk a mile and a half to start their journeys were long since past. The only way to have developed Calverley & Rodley

An oil lamp at Arthington about to be extinguished for the last time on 20 March 1965.
(John Holroyd)

station would have been as a park and ride facility involving complete rebuilding. Failing this there was a strong case for eliminating such a remote station in order to accelerate journeys between centres of population. When the axe fell in 1965 it was a blunt instrument which landed indiscriminately on services both with and without potential.

Had it survived, Apperley Bridge station would have benefited from the greater freedom and affluence of what would have now been the railcard holding students at Woodhouse Grove School. It could also have offered car parking for commuters from Rawdon and Yeadon. Nowadays almost all local stations have car parks but in the 1960s the BR attitude was that such facilities 'encouraged people to use cars!'

Another station to shut its doors on 20 March 1965 was Saltaire. The official story now is that the replacement wooden halt opened in 1984 is both an architectural and a commercial success. Manned only by a saver strip machine but with platforms the right height, proper illumination and a better train service, it is claimed to be doing worthwhile business. There were one or two of us who objected to its closure in the first place.

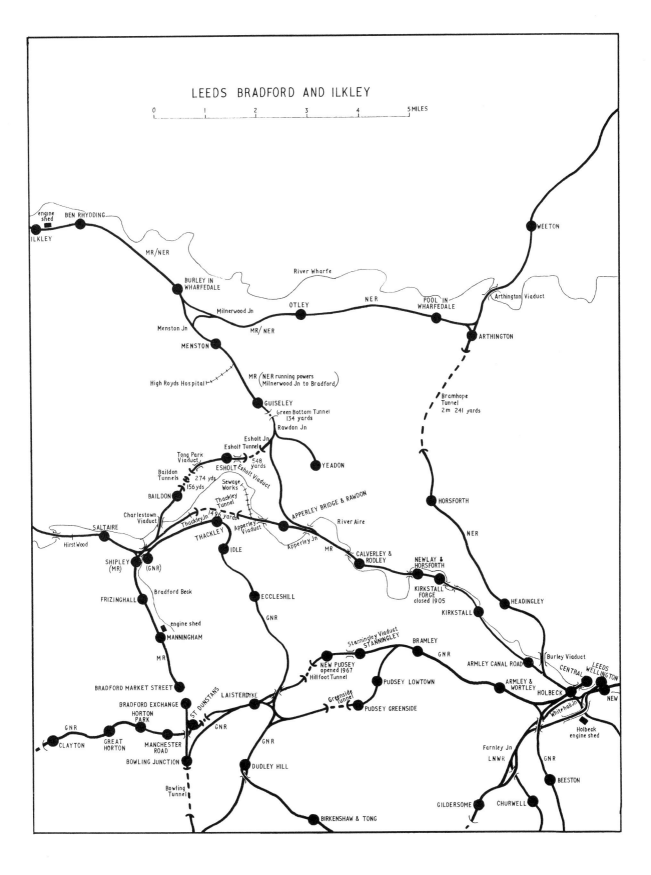

LEEDS BRADFORD AND ILKLEY

0   1   2   3   4   5 MILES

engine shed
ILKLEY
BEN RHYDDING
WEETON
MR/NER
River Wharfe
BURLEY IN WHARFEDALE
Milnerwood Jn
OTLEY
NER
POOL IN WHARFEDALE
Arthington Viaduct
Menston Jn
MR/NER
ARTHINGTON
MENSTON
High Royds Hospital
MR / NER running powers
(Milnerwood Jn to Bradford)
Bramhope Tunnel 2m 241 yards
GUISELEY
Green Bottom Tunnel 134 yards
Rawdon Jn
Esholt Jn
Esholt Tunnel
Tong Park Viaduct
548 yards
ESHOLT Esholt Viaduct
YEADON
Baildon Tunnels
274 yds
156 yds
Sewage Works
BAILDON
Thackley Tunnel 1496 yards
APPERLEY BRIDGE & RAWDON
HORSFORTH
Charlestown Viaduct
Thackley Jn
Apperley Viaduct
River Aire
NER
SALTAIRE
THACKLEY
Apperley Jn
Hirst Wood
IDLE
MR
CALVERLEY & RODLEY
NEWLAY & HORSFORTH
SHIPLEY (MR)   (GNR)
KIRKSTALL FORGE closed 1905
HEADINGLEY
Bradford Beck
ECCLESHILL
KIRKSTALL
FRIZINGHALL
GNR
engine shed
MANNINGHAM
Stanningley Viaduct STANNINGLEY
BRAMLEY
Burley Viaduct
MR
NEW PUDSEY opened 1967
Hillfoot Tunnel
GNR
ARMLEY CANAL ROAD
LEEDS CENTRAL WELLINGTON
BRADFORD MARKET STREET
PUDSEY LOWTOWN
ARMLEY & WORTLEY
ST DUNSTANS
LAISTERDYKE
Greenside Tunnel
PUDSEY GREENSIDE
HOLBECK
NEW
BRADFORD EXCHANGE
HORTON PARK
GNR
Whitehall Jn
GNR
CLAYTON
GREAT HORTON
MANCHESTER ROAD
GNR
GNR
Farnley Jn
LNWR
Holbeck engine shed
BOWLING JUNCTION
DUDLEY HILL
GNR
GNR
BEESTON
Bowling Tunnel
GILDERSOME
CHURWELL
BIRKENSHAW & TONG

A Journey Through Airedale

The present station at Leeds is not strictly the Leeds City traditionally used by Airedale trains. The Midland Railway had its terminus in Leeds at Wellington station which first brought trains into the centre of this city in 1846. Some 23 years later, the London & North Western and North Eastern companies, who had hitherto shared the facilities at Wellington, moved into their own premises at the adjacent Leeds New station. In 1938 Wellington and New were linked and renamed Leeds City but since 1967 all passenger services have used the former LNWR/NER part leaving Wellington as a parcels depot. Passengers may still use the entrance to Wellington station at the corner of City Square but are then subjected to walking through a narrow, fenced off part of the almost derelict and rather foul smelling concourse to reach the inhabited part of Leeds City station.

The present twelve platform passenger station is called upon to handle far more trains than was envisaged when the reorganisation was planned in the early 1960s. Both the station itself and the layout at its western end are somewhat congested at busy times.

The journey to Skipton can be made in either a diesel multiple unit or loco hauled train. Most of the latter variant are through from Hull to either Lancaster or Carlisle but with the odd exception they form part of the hourly interval service and call at all stations as far as Skipton.

At Leeds City East Junction, formerly Canal Junction, the line carrying local and Inter City trains to Wakefield, Doncaster and Kings Cross branches to the left and almost immediately runs onto Farnley Viaduct. Prior to 1967, when these ex Great Northern trains used Leeds Central station, Farnley viaduct carried the Huddersfield line.

Leeds City North Junction marks the divergence of the former Midland Railway's main lines to the North and South. Until 1967, expresses from St Pancras and the Midlands reversed at Leeds Wellington before continuing to Bradford Forster Square or the North via Skipton. Today the Midland route southwards carries only a local passenger service as far as Normanton. Even this is threatened with diversion via Wakefield Westgate. Its downfall can perhaps be attributed to George Stephenson's preference for lines which avoided gradients but which, unfortunately, tended to avoid centres of population as well.

At Whitehall Junction the curve from Engine Shed Junction, rarely used by passenger trains, trails in just before the ex LNWR route to Huddersfield and Manchester curves away to the left. Trains on the former Great Northern line to Bradford Exchange also diverge at this same point. Before 1967, they departed from Leeds Central and crossed over the Aire Valley line at the two level Holbeck Station. At Geldard Junction, a spur came down from Leeds Central allowing trains from that terminus to get onto the ex NER Harrogate line which then leaves the Aire Valley route a little further on at Wortley Junction.

From this point, the line to Shipley was reduced from quadruple to double track in 1967. Two years earlier the intermediate stations had closed and all five have been completely demolished. With all the goods yards, private sidings and most of the signalling also gone, the line between Leeds and Shipley would barely be recognisable today to somebody who knew it before the axe struck.

Armley Canal Road station, consisting of two long island platforms, stood in a cutting. At this point the 'fast' lines, the pair used mainly by passenger trains from Leeds to Bradford were on the north side. Between Armley and Kirkstall they crossed over the 'slow' lines thus avoiding conflict with the flow of freight traffic from the Midland Main line, south of Leeds towards Skipton. Something which used to confuse travellers was that almost all Leeds – Bradford locals used the 'fast' lines and were often overtaken by Leeds to Morecambe or Glasgow expresses travelling along the 'slow' lines. It was the 'fast' lines which were removed with 'dequadrification' in 1967.

Kirkstall Junction Signal Box is a reminder that the Midland Railway called anything a junction where there was so much of a cross over. There did not need to be a divergence of routes. Today the box marks the beginning of manual signalling after leaving the area controlled by Leeds power box. There are also goods loops on each side so that the few remaining freight trains can be overtaken.

Situated between Kirkstall and Newlay on the right hand side was Kirkstall Forge, served by a private railway system and, at one time, by a passenger station. This closed when the line was quadrupled in 1905 but remains of it were visible until the 1960s.

The line crosses the River Aire just after Newlay station then passes through a deep rock cutting part of which was a tunnel prior to quadrupling in 1904. Calverley & Rodley station was located beyond the bridge on Calverley Lane, a minor road about ¼ mile west of the Leeds Ring Road bridge. There were extensive sidings here on the Newlay side of the station which in later years stored excursion coaches on the north side and goods brake vans on the south side of the main line.

The approach to Apperley Junction is marked by a splitting distant. There used to be two of them when the 'fast' lines were also in use. This device, which is becoming increasingly rare, used to help keep on the move trains which would otherwise have had to slow down and virtually stop on the approach to a junction. Because the speed restriction for Ilkley trains is lower than for those going straight on to Shipley, an ordinary distant signal would have to be held at caution for Ilkley bound trains even when the route through Apperley Junction is clear.

Apperley Bridge Station was a mixture of old and new. Platform 4 on the up slow line (the northern most track) was shorter and lower than the other three and was surfaced with flagstones rather than gravel. Access to it was by a dark stone staircase rather than the wooden ones which linked the other platforms. This is because that part of the original station was not rebuilt when the railway was widened at the turn of the century. The station was gas lit to the end having acquired this facility at a very early stage, courtesy of the adjacent Woodhouse Grove School which supplied the gas from its own gasometer from about 1849.

When the line was quadrupled the additional tracks were laid on different sides at various stages of the route. In Apperley Bridge station the 'slow' lines were the originals but immediately on the Shipley side, they curve

The concourse of Leeds Wellington Station in July 1961.
(P. Sunderland)

to the right and the 'fast' lines then assumed the original course which before widening was dead straight from Apperley Junction to a point ½ mile into Thackley Tunnel.

The present Apperley Viaduct and Thackley Tunnel date from the quadrupling in 1901. Their older counterparts on the 'fast' lines stand disused alongside.

Between these two earthworks stood Apperley Viaduct signal box which was a block post on the 'slow' lines only and which controlled the sidings for Esholt Sewage Works. From 1910 until the mid 1970s, this utility had a private railway system for the internal movement of produce and for the despatch by rail of some which it was able to sell.

Beyond Thackley Tunnel, where the canal comes alongside, was Thackley Junction, a series of cross overs between 'fast' and 'slow' lines located near the site of a very early but short lived station serving Idle.

Directly opposite Guiseley Junction box, where the line from Ilkley trails in, there was a stone built Great Northern signal box called Shipley Junction which regulated movements around the Shipley terminus of the Great Northern branch from Bradford Exchange via Laisterdyke. Closed as long ago as 1931, the passenger station survives in the guise of a motor cycle shop. The failure to run GNR trains into the Midland station must have had something to do with the line's early demise. The GNR branch made physical connection with the Midland Railway at Leeds Junction signal box which stood at one corner of the Shipley triangle.

It took until 1979 to provide a platform on the 'main line' curve at Shipley. Even then it was done on the cheap and pasenger access from the town centre involves a walk of nearly half a mile. A ramp from the road bridge above Bingley Junction onto platform 5, which is the one used by most Shipley passengers, would correct this.

When Saltaire station was reopened in 1984, it was felt that something a little better than the standard wooden halt was required to remain in keeping with the environment of Sir Titus Salt's model village. So they still went ahead with a wooden halt but with the addition of imitation gas lamps, a full slate roof on top of the waiting shelters and Midland style diagonal fencing. The previous station on the same site was noted for its long low platforms, passengers requiring steps to board the trains.

A private siding served an iron foundry on the south side of the line at Hirst Wood ¾ mile beyond Saltaire.

A 151 yard tunnel leads immediately into Bingley station where the platforms have been shortened in recent years. This station dates from 1892, its predecessor having been a little further on near the Three Rise Lock. As the train pulls away from Bingley, the unique Five Rise Lock can be seen on the Leeds & Liverpool Canal beyond the Three Rise.

The route from Shipley to Skipton was never quadrupled throughout but from Bingley to Thwaites there were goods lines on the outside of the two passenger lines. These were removed in 1967. Crossflatts is a wooden halt opened in 1982 on a site where the Midland Railway always held out against building a station. That company did however yield to pressure for passenger facilities at Thwaites but found the response disappointing. There is no visible evidence now of the station which closed in 1909 after a life of 17 years.

Keighley station has two long platforms (1 and 2) on the main line and two rather shorter ones (3 and 4) on the Worth Valley branch. There was an unnumbered bay platform at the Shipley end of platform 1.

The Keighley & Worth Valley Railway climbs for 4¾ miles at a maximum of 1 in 56 to the Pennine village of Oxenhope. In common with many preserved railways, it operates a variety of motive power and rolling stock much of which would never have worked on this type of line in pre preservation days. However, it is possible to make the journey behind Ivatt 2 – 6 – 2T No. 41241 which is of the class which dominated the Worth Valley service during the 1950s. It is not however push-pull fitted.

The branch begins with a curve through more than 90 degrees on a gradient of 1 in 58 and heavy trains have always experienced difficulty getting started when the rails are greasy. Part way to Ingrow is the site of Keighley G N Junction where passenger trains to Halifax and Bradford Exchange crossed onto the Great Northern Railway which had started from its own goods depot now the Electricity Board premises near Keighley Station.

The former goods yard at Ingrow is now the KWVR boiler works. The station, which is now a request stop leads directly into the 150 yard tunnel.

The diminutive station at Damems once enjoyed goods facilities in the form of a single siding. The small signal box protecting the level crossing came from Earby on the closed Skipton to Colne line. A quarter mile further is Damems Junction which, in true Midland Railway tradition, describes just a passing loop. The signal box was obtained from Frizinghall after the KWVR decided to install a passing loop at this point. Until the 1950s there had been a loop through Oakworth station but there was no room for a second platform there. The old loop was not used to pass two passenger trains.

The line leaves Oakworth on an embankment. Below on the left hand side, now drained, is the former Vale Mill Dam over which the line crossed by a timber viaduct before the deviation was built in 1892.

At Haworth station a footbridge gives pedestrian access to the village which is reached by a steep cobbled road. Beyond this bridge on the left is the extensive goods yard which has been turned into the KWVR motive power depot. Part of the one time passing loop remains to give access into this yard.

The former goods yard at Oxenhope is now occupied by carriage sidings and by the Exhibition Shed which houses locomotives which are out of service but sufficiently presentable for public display. From Keighley the line has climbed 330 feet at an average gradient of 1 in 76, and unfitted goods trains are warned to stop and pin down their brakes before leaving Oxenhope.

Leaving Keighley for Skipton, the former Midland Railway goods yard has recently given way to a supermarket which has helped to move the shopping centre towards the station.

Keighley engine shed which used to house about three locomotives was situated on the right just beyond the next road bridge.

The terrain between Keighley and Skipton through the wide Aire Valley is undulating and the gradients are easy. Steeton & Silsden station was on the Skipton side of the level crossing which is still protected by Steeton Station signal box. Kildwick & Crosshills station was resited in 1889 from a position adjacent to the level crossing to a point ¼ mile nearer Skipton. At Cononley the platforms are still intact though the station, like the others, closed in 1965. The former Midland signal box was removed in 1964 in favour of a small cabin which protects the level crossing and acts as a block post with colour light signals.

For the last mile and a half into Skipton from Snaygill there were again four tracks. The Ilkley branch crosses by a viaduct just before the line curves to the left past the pre 1876 station and into the present structure. This has a main platform with a bay on the up (Leeds side) and an island platform on the down line. Platforms 5 and 6 were at a slightly higher level on the Ilkley and Grassington lines.

Following closure of the line to Ilkley in 1965, and the loss of the potentially very useful Colne line in 1970, Skipton has declined in importance. The bay and loop platforms are now without tracks and the subway leading to the Ilkley platforms is bricked up. Although the motive power depot closed in April 1967, the station remains a stabling point and a depot for drivers and guards.

4-4-0s Nos. 1011 and 565 at Leeds Wellington with the 'Thames – Forth Express' on 27 June 1936.

(G.H. Butland)

A Leeds City to Bradford Forster Square local passing the closed station at Holbeck in April 1961.
(P. Sunderland)

Holbeck Low Level on its last day, 5 July 1958.
(G.C. Lewthwaite)

4F 0-6-0 No. 44467 heads a partially fitted freight through the disused platforms at Holbeck Low Level in October 1963
(Martin Bairstow collection)

And through Wharfedale

One of the failings of the railway builders was their leaving cities such as Bradford with two dead end stations when one central installation would have been just as easy to accomplish in the days before the city centre had been built.

In 1967, BR attempted to concentrate all Bradford's passenger services on Exchange station but this was impossible as long as there remained a service to Ilkley. So, although main line trains were withdrawn from Forster Square station, two platforms were fenced off to serve the remaining dmus to Ilkley and Keighley whilst the rest of the station was given over to the exclusive handling of parcels.

When BR withdrew from the business of collecting and delivering parcels in 1981, Bradford Forster Square became even more a ghost station. The fleet of yellow road vehicles disappeared and in due course the tracks in platforms 3 to 6, the extensive sidings and the adjacent Valley goods depot all became derelict. Since 1984, the only operational tracks in the once expansive layout have been the double line which simply arrives from Shipley and runs into platforms 1 and 2. Signalling is remotely controlled by Shipley – Bradford Junction box.

There were formerly four tracks for passenger trains leaving Bradford Forster Square which were joined by the goods lines from Valley at Manningham Junction situated on the Bradford side of Queens Road bridge. From here to Shipley there were two passenger lines occupying the left hand side of the formation and serving Manningham and Frizinghall stations. The two goods lines ran on the right and continued round the back of Shipley station as far as Leeds Junction.

The motive power depot for Bradford was at Manningham alongside the station on the east side. Beyond the engine shed were the carriage sidings access to which was controlled by Manningham Sidings signal box which was on the left hand side of the main line half way to Frizinghall.

Passenger access to Frizinghall station was from the road bridge before the overhead buildings were demolished in the late 1950s and the booking office transferred to a converted waiting room on the up (Shipley bound) platform.

Shipley goods yard is still used by a scrap merchant and is now one of only two sources of rail freight in Airedale. There used to be a signal box at the Bradford end of the yard called Shipley Goods. The block sections were so short in this area that the lineside appeared saturated wth signals in many cases the distants for the box in front being underneath the home signals.

Today Shipley station appears incredibly bare. The canopies have been removed and platform 1, formerly used by Bradford to Keighley trains has no track. That side of the triangle was singled in 1980 but it has not been possible for trains to pass in platforms 1 and 2 since the introduction of bogie coaches because of the sharp curve and restricted clearance. Platform 3, now used only by Ilkley trains, was also the departure platform for Leeds. It used to be longer and, being on a right hand curve, it required a railman to relay the guard's signal to the driver. The occasion in 1964 when a guard missed his train was probably not the only time it happened. He had to venture so far from his van to get the driver to see his green lamp that he couldn't get back on again in time.

The Ilkley train leaves the Leeds line at Guiseley Junction. The track from here to Guiseley station was singled in 1983. A bridge over the canal is followed by Charlestown Viaduct which spans both the River Aire and the main road. Baildon station which was closed for 20 years retains its buildings on the main platform but they are not in railway use.

Two tunnels lead onto Tong Park Viaduct then the line passes by a bridge under Hollins Hill and through the site of Esholt station which closed in 1940 and was demolished in the early 1950s. The signals here were worked from a ground frame on the platform. Mr G H Butland recalls an incident from the 1920s. The station master had set the signals at danger following the departure of an all stations Ilkley to Bradford train and thought that he had sufficient time to pay a call before the Harrogate to Bradford train was due to pass. He was disturbed from reading his paper, or whatever he was doing in there, by the whistle of the LNER train which was not booked to stop at Esholt. He emerged with his trousers at half mast and made a dash for the ground frame.

After passing noisily through Esholt Tunnel, the train comes upon Esholt Junction where the line from Leeds joins. Since 1983, the two single lines have merely come alongside and run parallel to Guiseley station. Esholt Junction box has been removed and awaits a possible new life on the Worth Valley line at Keighley.

After leaving Apperley Junction, the Leeds – Ilkley trains run alongside the main line for a while then climb above the former Apperley Bridge goods yard, through short tunnels called Hindles and Apperley Lane then through woodlands overlooking Esholt Sewage Works. In modern times if Esholt Junction was not clear, trains were held by the home signal at the entrance to Springs Tunnel some way back from the junction. Before 1892, however, the home signal was located in the 'V' of the junction alongside the one for the line from Bradford. Disaster struck on the afternoon of 9 June 1892 when the 3.07 Leeds – Ilkley collided with the 3.10 Ilkley – Bradford as they negotiated the Junction. The 3.07 had been accepted by Esholt Junction box under the prevailing 'section clear but junction blocked' procedure. This meant that the train had to be stopped at Apperley Junction and then shown a green flag so that the driver could expect to be stopped again at Esholt Junction. It was therefore no surprise for him to find the Esholt Junction distant at caution but, on emerging from Springs Tunnel, he saw what he took to be the home signal at clear. In fact this was the signal for the line from Bradford which was about to be restored to danger following the passage of a North Eastern Bradford to Harrogate train. His own signal was obscured by a bush. There were five fatalities and numerous injuries.

¼ mile beyond Esholt Junction the short Yeadon branch trailed in at Rawdon Junction. This single track line climbed at a maximum of 1 in 50 for a distance of one mile. The passenger station was just beyond the bridge over Henshaw Lane. The line then continued into a headshunt to give access to the goods yard.

Still visible at Guiseley Station are the platform extensions which used to permit carriages to be set back to facilitate the remarshalling of trains which arrived from Bradford and from Leeds with portions for both Ilkley and

47142 with the 10.40 Carlisle to Leeds passes an Ilkley bound dmu at Wortley Junction on 13 August 1983. The Harrogate line branches to the right.   (G.W. Morrison)

Otley.

High Royds Hospital which stands to the west of the line between Guiseley and Menston had a private siding over half a mile in length. It was in use from 1883 until 1951 and was electrified in 1924.

The 38 yard Otley & Bradford Road Tunnel brings the line into Menston station. Half a mile further, at Menston Junction, the signal box was on the left opposite the point where the line to Otley began its 1 in 59 descent. Curving sharply to the right this line soon came alongside the Otley & Ilkley Joint line at the point where both crossed the Bradford to Ilkley main road but required further distance to lose height before joining it at Milnerwood Junction.

The buildings of Otley station were in similar style to those which can still be seen at Ilkley. They were situated on the Arthington bound platform which was connected by a subway to an island platform. Beyond Otley the line continued in North Eastern Railway ownership with the wide valley to the north but with the land rising steeply on the south side towards Otley Chevin.

Pool in Wharfedale station had staggered platforms, that on the down (Ilkley) side being an island.

At Arthington, the Otley branch joined the Leeds – Harrogate line by means of a triangular junction. The station, which closed with the Otley line in 1965 had platforms on the Leeds – Harrogate and Leeds – Otley sides of the layout. Before the branch opened, the station was located nearer to Harrogate where the Pool to Harewood road passes underneath the railway.

North Eastern trains from Ilkley and Otley to Leeds stopped in the sharply curved branch platforms at Arthington and then passed through the 2 mile 241 yard Bramhope Tunnel. After calling at Horsforth and Headingley stations, they came alongside the Midland Railway at Wortley Junction then proceeded through Holbeck Low Level to reach Leeds New station. It is hoped that a more detailed description of this route will form part of a future book on the railways of Harrogate.

Returning to Wharfedale, the Midland route from

Guiseley and the Joint Line from Otley came together at Burley Junction, a short distance before Burley in Wharfedale station. Burley Junction signal box remains in use with semaphore signals, the only ones now on the Ilkley line, simply to divide the section between Guiseley and Ilkley. There is no longer even a cross over between up and down lines to justify retention of the term 'junction'. New housing has been built on the site of the former goods yard on the right hand side of the line, hopefully, increasing the numbers of potential commuters.

For the remaining 3½ miles to Ilkley, the line clings to the hillside overlooking Wharfedale. The 'Cow and Calf' rocks can be seen on Ilkley Moor above Ben Rhydding station.

The two platforms now in use at Ilkley comprise the original Otley & Ilkley Joint station of 1865 before the Skipton line was built. A supermarket now occupies the site of the goods yards whilst commuters park their cars on the former carriage sidings behind platform 1 which were the site of the pre-1892 engine shed. The replacement shed was situated on the north side of the line towards Ben Rhydding.

The Midland Railway line to Skipton left the Otley & Ilkley Joint at Ilkley Junction at the entrance to the station then passed through platforms 3 and 4 on a rising gradient. It crossed Brook Street by a girder bridge and was then carried through the town on a 25 arch viaduct.

The village of Addingham was served by a stone built station. From here the line climbed at 1 in 110 for one mile then began to descend at 1 in 120 towards Bolton Abbey where the wooden station buildings were on the Ilkley bound platform.

The summit of the line was reached after climbing for two miles at 1 in 110 then a short level stretch preceded the descent towards Skipton. On the approach to Embsay, there was a siding to serve the Skipton Rock Company whose private 'railway' system pre-dated the main line railways and fed into a branch of the Leeds & Liverpool Canal at Skipton. Built originally to a gauge of 4ft 1in, it was rebuilt to standard after the Ilkley to Skipton line opened but fell into disuse after 1947.

At Embsay Junction, the line from Ilkley was joined by the Grassington branch for the final descent at 1 in 85

through Haw Bank Tunnel and then on an embankment to reach Skipton by a long curve. A viaduct across the canal, road and Aire Valley railway brings the Ilkley branch into platforms 5 and 6 of Skipton station. These are slightly elevated from the rest of the station. The physical connection is at Skipton Station North Junction.

The Grassington branch remains in use as far as Swinden Lime Works, situated midway between Rylstone and Grassington stations. The branch was always single track from Embsay Junction though since closure of the Ilkley line, the section from Skipton to Embsay Junction has also been reduced to a single line.

The sole intermediate station at Rylstone was inconveniently sited. The line passes closer to the village and to nearby Hetton at a point ½ mile nearer to Skipton. Presumably the Yorkshire Dales Railway preferred a site near a level crossing to one on an embankment. There was at one time a passing loop at Rylstone which had just one platform and wooden buildings very similar to those at Grassington.

Grassington & Threshfield station stood midway between the two villages and proved so vulnerable to the introduction of bus services running direct into the centre of Grassington. It had two platforms with the buildings situated on the right hand one looking towards the buffer stops. The signal box was located on the west side to the south of the platforms from where it controlled access to the goods yard on the right hand side and to Delaney's stone siding which curved sharply to the left and ran for about 1 mile towards a quarry.

Embsay station is now the home of the Yorkshire Dales Railway Trust which seeks to rebuild the railway thence to Bolton Abbey. But although the Trust owns the section between Embsay station and Embsay Junction, it does not hold serious hope of ever operating to Skipton. Experience in the railway preservation world is that as long as BR operate that line, there is no practical chance of anybody else being able to run trains over it. If the stone traffic from Swinden Lime Works ever ceased, the heavily engineered route into Skipton would become available but would present a formidable task for preservation.

Between Armley and Kirkstall, the 'fast' lines crossed over the 'slow'. The view is towards Leeds on 22 June 1964.

(Peter E. Baughan)

4-6-0 No. 45569 'Tasmania' passing Kirkstall with a Glasgow to St Pancras express on 3 July 1960. *(D. Butterfield)*

The remains of Kirkstall Forge Station which closed in 1905, seen on 22 June 1964 looking south. *(Peter E. Baughan)*

The 13.30 Leeds to Morecambe dmu passes through the closed station at Newlay & Horsforth on 6 August 1966. *(M. Mitchell)*

25056 and 25060 head a Carlisle to Harrogate special through Rodley Cutting, between Calverley & Rodley and Newlay, on 30 July 1980. *(G.W. Morrison)*

8F 2-8-0 No 48652 passes Calverley & Rodley on the up slow line with a train of empty mineral wagons on 16 April 1961. *(G.W. Morrison)*

4-4-0 No. 41071 draws into platform 3 at Calverley & Rodley as a two coach local prepares to leave for Leeds on 27 May 1957. *(J.C.W. Halliday)*

2-6-4T No. 42141 passing through platform 1 at Apperley Bridge & Rawdon about 1960.
(J.C.W. Halliday)

4F 0-6-0 No. 43871 with a northbound freight at Apperley Bridge on 21 July 1955.
(J.C.W. Halliday)

The south end of Thackley Tunnel about 1906. The signal box is disused having been open only from 1898 to 1902. The quadruple track meant that it was no longer necessary to split the block section on the fast line.
(J.H. Wright, courtesy Robin Higgins)

The north end of Thackley Tunnel about 1906 when the slow lines, on the left, were relatively new.

(J.H. Wright, courtesy Robin Higgins)

The 11.35 Leeds to Skipton between Thackley and Guiseley Junctions on 9 October 1978. This section remained four track until 1980.

(G.W. Morrison)

Newly refurbished Metro-Cammell units pass at Guiseley Junction on 22 June 1979. *(G.W. Morrison)*

2P 4-4-0 No. 40409 arrives at Shipley with a Leeds to Bradford fast service on 18 June 1957.

(J.C.W. Halliday)

Construction and Development

The Leeds & Bradford Railway

The first eleven miles of railway through the Aire Valley as far as Shipley were conceived as a link between the cities of Leeds and Bradford. Leeds had enjoyed the benefit of railway communication since 1834 when the Leeds & Selby Railway had opened from a terminus at Marsh Lane in the east end of the city. The opening on 1 July 1840 of the North Midland Railway placed Leeds at the end of a continuous line from London and from the Midlands.

Bradford was already established as the centre of the wool textile industry but was nine miles from the nearest railway facilities either at Leeds or at 'Brighouse for Bradford' station in the Calder Valley.

There were two routes by which a railway might be built between Leeds and Bradford. The early 1830s had seen the unsuccessful promotion of a 'short line' which would have taken a direct course via Stanningley involving gradients of the order of 1 in 50. The alternative to the 'short line' was a 'valley line' following the route of the canal via Shipley. The distance would be 13½ miles but the gradients relatively easy. The 'valley line' was favoured by George Stephenson who had surveyed a route in 1838 whilst working on the North Midland project.

On 22 December 1843, a provisional committee was formed to manage the affairs of the Leeds & Bradford Railway Company pending its formal incorporation by Act of Parliament on 4 July 1844. The chairman was George Hudson, the 'Railway King'.

This gentleman, who lived from 1800 until 1871, became one of the richest men in York following the death of an uncle in 1827. Hudson used his wealth both to indulge himself and to bribe his way into local politics. He became Lord Mayor of York in 1838 and eventually entered Parliament as member for Sunderland in 1845. Meanwhile he had acquired an interest in railways becoming the first chairman of the York & North Midland Railway in 1836.

By the mid 1840s, a quarter of the country's railways were under Hudson's control. The largest component in Hudson's empire was the Midland Railway, formed in 1844 by the amalgamation of the North Midland, Midland Counties and Derby & Birmingham Junction Railways which together stretched from the Midlands to Leeds.

It would have been logical for the Leeds & Bradford Railway to have been viewed as an extension of the Midland especially with Hudson as its chairman and Stephenson as engineer. Amalgamation did follow in 1846 but the circumstances by which this was achieved proved to be a turning point in the career of Hudson leading to his 'dethronement' in 1848.

On 30 December 1843, the Provisional Committee of the Leeds & Bradford Railway met to allot shares. These had been oversubscribed and the numbers allotted to most applicants were scaled down but Hudson and his deputy chairman, John Waddingham, made sure that they got the numbers they wanted. The shares would then immediately acquire a premium value leaving it open to Hudson and his associate to make a very substantial capital gain.

Construction work began immediately on receiving Parliamentary sanction in July 1844 and was completed in just under two years. The official opening on 30 June 1846 was marked by a public holiday in Bradford. The Leeds terminus at Wellington Station was also used by Midland Railway trains from 1 July 1846.

In common with many contemporary railways, the Leeds & Bradford was opened at the first opportunity. The company was anxious to get trains moving and income flowing almost as soon as the track was laid. The provision of intermediate stations had to come later. For about a fortnight all trains ran non stop then temporary arrangements were made for a station at Shipley. By the end of July, Apperley Bridge, Calverley Bridge (as it was then called) and Kirkstall had all appeared in the timetable. Newlay came later in 1846 and Armley the following year. Permanent structures were eventually provided at all these but not at the short lived Idle station. This appears to have lasted about 12 months between September 1847 and September 1848. It was the result of pressure from the village of Idle for a station at the west end of Thackley Tunnel. It was evidently not a success.

In order to win support for its 1844 Bill, the Leeds & Bradford Railway had committed itself to extensions from Shipley to Keighley and from Bradford to Halifax. As regards Keighley, the company quickly honoured its obligation.

Events concerning the Halifax proposal were rather more complicated. A nominally independent West Yorkshire Railway, backed by the Leeds & Bradford, was promoted to run from Bradford through Halifax to Sowerby Bridge in the Calder Valley. Here it would join the Manchester & Leeds Railway which responded by sponsoring the Leeds & West Riding Junction Railway, a rival scheme involving a network of lines around the West Riding more fully described in the 'Calder Valley' book. Part of the project was an alternative to the West Yorkshire Railway. Linking Sowerby Bridge, Halifax, Bradford and Leeds, it differed from its rival by adopting the 'short line' between Bradford and Leeds via Stanningley.

The West Yorkshire and Leeds & West Riding Junction schemes both went before Parliament in 1845 and were both rejected. The Manchester & Leeds Railway then proposed amalgamation with the Leeds & Bradford. This offer was accepted by Hudson and a detailed agreement reached in November 1845. It was proposed that the link between Sowerby Bridge and Bradford would be built and the Leeds & Bradford Railway would then be part of the Manchester to Leeds main line.

The Midland Railway may have wondered what its chairman was doing giving the Leeds & Bradford line to a company which was outside the Hudson Empire and not on particularly good terms with the Midland. Hudson evidently had second thoughts and in June 1846 broke off the amalgamation, blaming the Manchester & Leeds for deviating from the agreed terms, and offered the Leeds & Bradford to the Midland Railway on terms which were excessive but benefited him personally. He then took the chair at a general meeting of Midland Railway shareholders and spoke and voted in favour of the deal.

This event marked the beginning of the decline of Hudson's power as his dealings began to come under closer scrutiny. It also condemned Bradford Midland

Station (the name Forster Square was not used until 1924) to remain a dead end with no connection to Bradford's other railways. The Manchester & Leeds Railway reached Bradford Exchange in 1850 but dropped plans to connect with the Leeds & Bradford line. Instead from 1854, its trains reached Leeds via the Leeds, Bradford & Halifax Junction Railway – the rival 'short line'.

Shipley to Skipton

Work on the line to Keighley and Skipton proceeded quickly and a locomotive was able to travel to Keighley on 13 February 1847. A Board of Trade inspection was carried out by Captain Simmons on 13 March and the public opening took place on Tuesday 16 March. Captain Simmons was back on 28 August as a single track was available between Keighley and Skipton. Following his approval and a directors special trip on 1 September, the line was opened to the public on Tuesday 7 September. By December, a second track was in use along with intermediate stations at Steeton, Kildwick and Cononley.

At this stage Skipton was a dead end but from 2 October 1848, the Midland Railway extended to Colne. On 1 February 1849, this town was also reached by the East Lancashire Railway from Burnley and from 2 April that year it became possible to get from Leeds to Liverpool via Skipton and Colne.

The 'Little' North Western Railway, soon to become part of the Midland, opened from Skipton to Clapham on 30 July 1849 and within a year the route to Lancaster and Morecambe was in use throughout. The line through Airedale became part of the Midland route to Scotland with the opening of the Clapham to Lowgill line on 1 October 1861. The Midland Railway's control over this route ended at Ingleton. Dissatisfaction at the handling of its traffic thence to Carlisle by the London & North Western Railway was a major factor in determining the Midland to construct the Settle & Carlisle line which finally opened to passenger traffic on 1 May 1876.

Early Schemes in Wharfedale

The River Wharfe is crossed at Arthington by the railway from Leeds to Harrogate. This line began life as the Leeds & Thirsk Railway which was incorporated in 1845 and opened in stages during 1848 and 1849.

In 1846, an Act was passed for a railway through Wharfedale itself. A company called the Lancashire & Yorkshire North Eastern Railway later changed its name to the 'Wharfdale' Railway (there was no e in Wharfedale at that time). The proposal had been to run from Skipton to York but the section east of Arthington was dropped at the Parliamentary stage. The 'Wharfdale' was to be leased to the Leeds & Thirsk and might have stood more chance of being built if it had stuck to that proposal. However the arrangement was broken off in November 1846 when a majority of 'Wharfdale' shareholders decided that they should take an independent course. At their half yearly meeting in Leeds on 23 February 1847, hopes were held of the line being opened concurrently with the Leeds & Thirsk. Such optimism proved unfounded. The 'Wharfdale' scheme was abandoned in 1852 after failing to get help from any of the established neighbouring railways.

In 1856, a fresh attempt was made by promoters of a Wharfedale Railway to gain the backing either of the Midland Railway or of the North Eastern (successor to the Leeds & Thirsk). Neither company was interested.

The Otley & Ilkley Joint Railway

During 1860 the Midland and North Eastern companies discussed the possibility of making a joint venture into Wharfedale, dispensing with any local promoters. The Midland was to build a branch from a junction near Apperley Bridge to Burley in Wharfedale, the North Eastern was to extend from Arthington to Otley and six miles of joint line were to link Otley and Ilkley. To conclude the agreement, the Midland undertook not to promote any new lines east of Otley and the North Eastern agreed not to do anything west of Ilkley. 11 July 1861 saw the passing of both the Midland and North Eastern Acts authorising their respective parts of the Otley & Ilkley Railway.

The town of Otley was en fête on 1 February 1865 when the first train arrived from Leeds at 7.38 am. Problems of land slips delayed the opening to Ilkley for a further six months. On 1 August both Midland and North Eastern trains began running into Ilkley to the accompaniment of brass bands.

At Arthington, the Otley and Ilkley line met the Leeds & Thirsk by a triangular junction. The station, which had previously been to the north of this point was resited with platforms on the Leeds – Otley and Leeds – Thirsk sides of the triangle. Another triangular layout was to be found between Menston, Burley and Milnerwood Junctions. The Burley to Milnerwood leg of this was part of the Otley & Ilkley Joint line but the other two curves were exclusively Midland property.

At Apperley Junction, the connection with the main line faced Leeds and it was necessary for trains from Bradford to reverse direction. The arrangements were anything but satisfactory and there was constant pressure voiced in the local press for a direct route from Bradford to Otley and Ilkley.

The Keighley & Worth Valley Railway

Three and a half miles to the south of Keighley lies the village of Haworth, well known for its association with the Brontë family. Members of the family invested in early railways and Branwell Brontë secured employment for a short time on the Manchester & Leeds Railway. Although none of them lived long enough to see the railway reach Haworth, they have, for over a century, posthumously helped to sustain the level of passenger traffic on the Worth Valley line by keeping up the numbers of tourists.

The 'Railway Mania' year of 1845 saw the proposed Manchester, Hebden Bridge & Keighley Junction Railway which was to link the Manchester & Leeds Railway at Hebden Bridge with the Leeds & Bradford at Keighley. The route would have been 12 miles in length and would have involved a long tunnel under Oxenhope Moor. Nothing came of it.

October 1861 brought a deputation of local businessmen to the Midland Railway headquarters at Derby. Agreement was reached that a local company would build a branch line from Keighley to Oxenhope which the Midland Railway would work. The track was to be single but sufficient land was to be purchased to allow doubling at a later date.

The Act was passed in June 1862 but work did not

begin until February 1864. Progress was frustrated by subsidence in Ingrow Tunnel and, on 14 November 1866, by flooding. The contractor had been able to run a train to Oxenhope and back on 1 November but a fortnight later found 40 yards of embankment near Damems had been washed away leaving the track suspended. Other damage had been sustained and it took until Saturday 13 April 1867 for the public opening to take place. This was a wet day and the first train failed to get to grips with the 1 in 58 gradient out of Keighley.

The branch always remained single except for the first ¾ mile out of Keighley which was doubled as part of the arrangements for bringing the Great Northern Railway into Keighley in 1884. A new Keighley Station on the Leeds side of the Bradford Road bridge was opened on 6 May 1883 with separate platforms at an angle for Worth Valley and the future Great Northern trains. Previously the station had been on the Skipton side of Bradford Road which prior to 1879 had crossed the railway by a level crossing.

Before finalising arrangements with the Great Northern Railway for use of part of the Worth Valley branch, the Midland had absorbed the Keighley & Worth Valley Railway from 1 July 1881. In this and other instances, the use of a local company to build a branch line was, for the main line railway, just a method of getting the branch built on the cheap. The KWVR company provided the capital and took all the risks. Then, when convenient the Midland took over the line at a discount.

For the first 25 years trains used a timber viaduct to cross the Vale Mill dam south of Oakworth. This was replaced in 1892 by a deviation involving an embankment, a three arch viaduct, several bridges and the short Mytholmes Tunnel.

Problems at Apperley Viaduct

The embryonic Worth Valley line was not the only victim of the floods which hit West Yorkshire on 14 November 1866. The Midland Railway company was far more concerned with the destruction of Apperley Viaduct which severed Bradford, Skipton and all points north from the remainder of the Midland system.

A 'Bradford Observer' reporter travelled by the 1 pm train from Bradford to Otley. Instead of the 49 minutes allowed in the timetable the journey consumed three hours. The train had to make two attempts at the ascent from Apperley Junction to Guiseley. It eventually succeeded by the wrong line, the other track being blocked by an embankment slip. On the return journey the train got no further than Apperley Bridge station because that viaduct carrying the line over the River Aire had disappeared.

The Apperley Bridge station master was advised by the guard of the 4.50 pm Bradford to Leeds train that the viaduct appeared insecure. The station master set off on foot and was able to halt an up goods train. The driver of the train, which consisted of an engine, tender, two wagons and a guard's van, saw the station master's handlamp as he emerged from Thackley tunnel and brought the train to a stand on the viaduct. The level of the River Aire had risen considerably and was flowing through all ten arches of the viaduct instead of the usual three. According to a newspaper correspondent signing himself 'Eye witness' the train stood on the viaduct for fifteen minutes whilst the crew and the station master debated what to do. The decision was made for them when the viaduct collapsed. The engine and tender became embedded in the river whilst the van and wagons flowed downstream. Passengers who were stranded at Apperley Bridge must have faced a difficult journey home. The railway to Leeds was under three feet of water at Kirkstall whilst the road to Bradford was flooded where it crosses the River Aire below the station.

For the next week trains were terminated at Shipley and Apperley Bridge. Through passengers travelled by the Great Northern Railway from Leeds Central to Bradford Adolphus Street whence they walked to the Midland station. An editorial in the 'Bradford Observer' claimed that the Midland Railway had received just retribution for its failure to build a joint station in Bradford with the other railway companies. Various correspondents agreed and one, pursuing a similar theme, stated that the Midland Railway would have been spared the disruption to its traffic if it had built a proper route from Bradford to Ilkley as trains could have been diverted via Guiseley.

From 24 November trains reverted to the normal time-

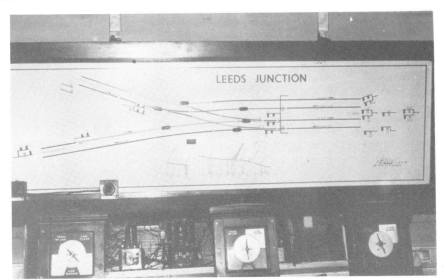

The block diagram inside Leeds Junction Signal Box (Shipley) on 23 April 1975 shortly before closure of the box.
(Stuart Baker)

table but terminated at either side of Apperley Viaduct where passengers crossed a footbridge. A replacement viaduct was opened on 3 January 1867 only six weeks after the disaster occured.

Shipley to Guiseley

In order to offer a direct route between Bradford and Wharfedale, the Midland Railway obtained powers in 1872 for a 3 ½ mile double track line commencing at Guiseley Junction, near Shipley, and running over three viaducts and through three tunnels to reach Esholt Junction, near Guiseley.

The line, which opened on 4 December 1876 offered the most direct route between Harrogate and Bradford and running powers were granted to the North Eastern Railway from Milnerwood Junction to Bradford.

Ilkley to Skipton

Prompted possibly by local attempts to promote a link between Ilkley and Skipton, the Midland Railway assumed the initiative and obtained the necessary powers by an Act of 16 July 1883. Work started in April 1885 and it was possible to open as far as Bolton Abbey on 16 May 1888. The remaining six miles to Skipton opened on 1 October the same year.

During the First World War, one track was removed between Addingham and Embsay, probably for use in building military railways in France. A passing loop was retained at Bolton Abbey. Double line working resumed in 1921 although the traffic could have been accommodated on a single line.

Guiseley to Yeadon

In 1881 the promoters of a Leeds & Yeadon District Railway approached the North Eastern Railway with plans for a line from Headingley to Guiseley. Intermediate stations would serve Horsforth, Rawdon and Yeadon. The NER gave the stock answer that it could not support any new line in Wharfedale without the consent of the Midland Railway. The latter company sent its chairman and general manager to a public meeting at Yeadon Town Hall on 10 November 1883. They advised that if the project were restricted to a Guiseley to Yeadon branch, the Midland Railway would not oppose it and would be prepared to work the line on completion.

The Guiseley, Yeadon & Rawdon Act was passed on 16 July 1885. The necessary capital could not be raised locally and the company required a loan from the Midland

Railway. In 1893, the partially completed line was purchased by the Midland.

Goods traffic commenced on 26 February 1894. Although a passenger station was provided at Yeadon, no regular service ever operated but there were occasional excursions.

An extension was authorised in 1891 from Yeadon to join the NER by a flying junction north of Headingley but sufficient capital was not forthcoming and the project was abandoned.

The Yorkshire Dales Railway

This railway, authorised in 1897 was a scaled down version of earlier, unsuccessful schemes to build a railway through Upper Wharfedale. Instead of aiming for Darlington, the Yorkshire Dales Railway decided to be content with a route from Embsay Junction to a point midway between the villages of Grassington and Threshfield.

The single track branch was worked by the Midland Railway from its opening on 29 July 1902 but the Yorkshire Dales Railway Company remained in existence until it was absorbed by the LMSR at the 1923 grouping. A passing loop was provided at Rylstone in 1904 when electric token working was introduced.

The Bradford Through Line

In 1898 the Midland Railway embarked upon its West Riding Lines which were intended to bring its trains into Dewsbury, Huddersfield and Halifax. As explained in the 'Standedge' book, the link from the Midland Main Line at Royston to the Calder Valley near Horbury was opened in 1905 and Midland branches were built into Dewsbury and Huddersfield. These ended up as little more than goods sidings and the centre piece of the West Riding Lines was never built. This would have left the Lancashire & Yorkshire Railway in the Spen Valley between Cleckheaton and Low Moor, would have passed through a tunnel at Bowling then crossed the centre of Bradford on a viaduct. After serving high level platforms at Market Street (Forster Square) Station, it would have dropped down to the level of the existing railway before Manningham. The Midland would have exercised running powers between Horbury and Cleckheaton and would have been able to route some London to Scotland traffic via Bradford. The project was postponed on the outbreak of the First World War and never resumed.

Shipley Station looking towards Bradford before rebuilding in 1875. *(D. Burrows collection)*

A class 104 unit leaves Shipley with a Bradford Forster Square to Keighley working on 23 June 1975.

(Stuart Baker)

45692 'Cyclops' approaching Saltaire with the afternoon slow from Bradford Forster Square to Carlisle in 1962.

(Richard Smithies)

'Britannia' 4-6-2 No. 70044 'Earl Haig' passing Saltaire with the northbound 'Thames – Clyde Express' on 3 January 1959.
(D. Butterfield)

Class 40 No. D200 calls at the rebuilt Saltaire Station with a Carlisle to Leeds service on 5 April 1985.
(Martin Bairstow)

4-6-2 No. 72008 'Clan McLeod' passing Hirst Wood with the all stations Bradford to Carlisle on 13 August 1965.
(Richard Smithies)

Midland Railway 4-4-0 No. 1577 calls at Bingley with an afternon Skipton train on 15 April 1905.
(J.H. Wright courtesy Robin Higgins)

The 15.08 Skipton to Bradford Forster Square local restarts from Bingley on 22 June 1964. *(Peter E. Baughan)*

D5235 brings the 12.30 Morecambe to Leeds into Bingley on 29 May 1965.   *(D. Butterfield)*

Bingley Station stood in front of the Three Rise Lock prior to the opening of the present station on 24 July 1892.
(Bingley Library)

'Crab' 2-6-0 No. 42762
approaching Bingley with an up
express on 19 August 1961.
        (Martin Bairstow collection)

A class 2P 4-4-0 passing the
site of the present Crossflatts
Station with a Carlisle to Leeds
express on 27 August 1907.
                (J.H. Wright,
        courtesy Robin Higgins)

4-6-0 No. 5050 travelling
towards Keighley along the four
track section west of Crossflatts
in 1948.   (W.H. Foster,
        courtesy John Holroyd)

45647 'Sturdee' comes off the goods line at Thwaites Junction on 15 April 1967 with a Leeds – Carnforth freight. *(G.W. Morrison)*

41325 standing in the bay platform at the south end of Keighley Station in 1960. The Worth Valley push-pull set also made trips to Bradford. *(P. Sunderland)*

A 'Black five' 4-6-0 passing Keighley South box at the approach to the station with a Morecambe train in the 1950s.
(Roy Brook)

'Jubilee' 4-6-0 No. 45647 'Sturdee' approaching Keighley with a Carlisle bound freight on 15 April 1967.   (P. Hutchinson)

A 3 car Metro Cammell set crosses onto the up line at Keighley before returning to Bradford in March 1980.
(Martin Bairstow)

A Derby built dmu stands in platform 4 at Keighley during the 18 month period that the Worth Valley service was dmu operated.   *(P. Sunderland)*

41273 arrives at Keighley with the Worth Valley push-pull service on Keighley Gala day in June 1957. The former Great Northern goods depot is behind the train.   *(P. Sunderland)*

An Oxenhope to Keighley push-pull service at Keighley GN Junction in July 1955.
(P. Sunderland)

A Keighley to Oxenhope dmu passing the closed station at Damems on 27 August 1960.
(Martin Bairstow collection)

Oakworth Station looking towards Keighley in July 1955.
(P. Sunderland)

41325 near Mytholmes in July 1955 with an Oxenhope train.　　　　　　　　*(P. Sunderland)*

Standard 2-6-2T No. 84009 propelling an Oxenhope to Keighley train out of Haworth in June 1957.

(P. Sunderland)

Haworth Station on 1 May 1965. The late Edgar Chapman, Vice Chairman, promotes a 'win a car' competition in aid of the struggling society.
(G.C. Lewthwaite)

3F 0-6-0 No. 43586 shunts at Haworth early in 1962.
(J.C.W. Halliday)

Haworth signal box shortly before demolition in 1956.
(P. Sunderland)

41325 stands at Oxenhope with the branch push-pull on 27 April 1957.   *(J.C.W. Halliday)*

The last day of BR passenger service at Oxenhope on 30 December 1961.   *(J.C.W. Halliday)*

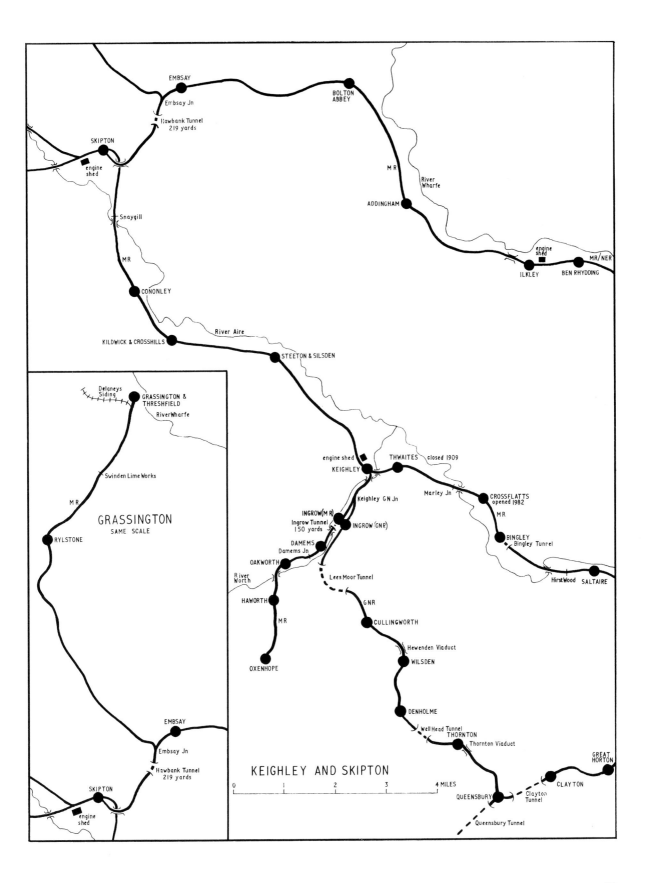

EMBSAY

Embsay Jn

Hawbank Tunnel
219 yards

BOLTON
ABBEY

SKIPTON

engine
shed

M R

River
Wharfe

Snaygill

ADDINGHAM

M R

CONONLEY

engine
shed

MR/NER

ILKLEY   BEN RHYDDING

River Aire

KILDWICK & CROSSHILLS

STEETON & SILSDEN

Delaneys
Siding

GRASSINGTON &
THRESHFIELD

RiverWharfe

engine shed

THWAITES   closed 1909

Swinden Lime Works

KEIGHLEY

CROSSFLATTS
opened 1982

M R

GRASSINGTON

SAME SCALE

Marley Jn

M R

Keighley GN Jn

RYLSTONE

INGROW(MR)

BINGLEY

Bingley Tunnel

Ingrow Tunnel
150 yards

INGROW (GNR)

DAMEMS

Damems Jn

OAKWORTH

HirstWood   SALTAIRE

River
Worth

Lees Moor Tunnel

HAWORTH

G N R

M R

CULLINGWORTH

Hewenden Viaduct

OXENHOPE

WILSDEN

EMBSAY

DENHOLME

Embsay Jn

Well Head Tunnel
THORNTON

Hawbank Tunnel
219 yards

Thornton Viaduct

GREAT
HORTON

SKIPTON

engine
shed

KEIGHLEY AND SKIPTON

CLAYTON

Clayton
Tunnel

QUEENSBURY

0   1   2   3   4 MILES

Queensbury Tunnel

8F 2-8-0 No. 48533 heads a train of empty mineral wagons through Keighley towards Skipton in June 1953.

(J. Davenport)

4-6-0 No. 45018 approaching Steeton & Silsden with a Bradford to Carlisle stopping service on 13 April 1962.

(G.W. Morrison)

Kildwick & Crosshills Station looking towards Skipton on 20 February 1965.

(G.C. Lewthwaite)

'Jubilee' class 4-6-0 No. 45697 'Achilles' between Kildwick and Cononley with a down express on 17 July 1965.

(Ian G. Holt)

Work in progress at Cononley as a Skipton to Bradford local calls at the station on 29 May 1960.

(D. Butterfield)

A compound 4-4-0 heads a Bradford via Ilkley train out of Skipton as 2-6-2T No. 41284 leaves with a local via Keighley in April 1958. *(P. Sunderland)*

4-6-0 No. 45273 on a Heysham to Leeds parcels train at Skipton in June 1967. *(J. Davenport)*

D25 with the 10.25 Leeds – Glasgow at Skipton on 7 July 1965. The Ilkley branch platforms 5 and 6 are on the extreme right.
(M. Mitchell)

KEIGHLEY TO OXENHOPE

MIDLAND RAILWAY

WEEKDAYS	am	am	am	am	am	am	SO am	SX pm	SO pm	pm	pm	SO pm	SX pm	pm	pm	pm	pm	pm	SO pm	SX pm	SO pm	pm
KEIGHLEY	5 25	7 33	8 06	9 10	9 11	10 18	12 20	12 00	12 05	1 55	2 50	3 37	4 48	5 35	6 10	6 57	7 52	8 55	9 43	10 10	10 50	11 35
INGROW	5 29	7 37	8 10	9 13		12 22	12 24	04	09	1 59	2 53	3 41	4 52	5 40	6 14	7 01	7 56	8 59	9 49	10 14	10 54	11 39
DAMEMS	5 32	7 40	—	—	11 25	12 27	11 07	12 2	02	2 58	3 44	5 43	6 17	7 59	9 02	9 52	10 17	10 57				
OAKWORTH	5 35	7 43	8 14	9 18	11 28	12 30	10	15	2 05	3 01	3 47	4 58	5 46	6 20	7 06	8 02	9 05	9 55	10 20	11 00	11 43	
HAWORTH	5 39	7 47	8 18	9 22	11 32	12 34	14	19	2 09	3 05	3 53	5 02	5 50	6 24	7 09	8 06	9 09	10 03	10 24	11 04	11 47	
OXENHOPE	5 42	7 50	8 21	9 25	11 35	12 37	17	22	2 12	3 08	3 54	5 06	5 53	6 27	7 12	8 09	9 13	10 03	10 27	11 07	11 50	

SUNDAYS

	am	am	pm	pm	pm	pm	pm	pm
KEIGHLEY	7 00	10 50	1 55	2 50	5 15	7 40	9 06
INGROW	7 04	10 54	1 59	2 54	5 19	7 44	9 10
DAMEMS	7 08	10 58	2 03	2 58	5 23	7 48	9 14
OAKWORTH	7 11	11 02	2 07	3 02	5 27	7 52	9 18
HAWORTH	7 15	11 06	2 11	3 06	5 31	7 56	9 22
OXENHOPE	7 18						

WEEKDAYS	am	am	am	am	am	am	am	pm	SO pm	pm	pm	pm	SO pm	SX pm	pm	SX pm	pm	pm	pm	SO pm	SX pm	SO pm	pm
OXENHOPE	5 07	5 48	6 53	7 55	8 26	9 32	10 50	11 40	12 43	2 18	3 13	3 54	4 03	5 12	5 57	6 35	7 17	8 18	9 20	10 10	10 32	13	
HAWORTH	5 10	5 16	6 56	7 58	8 29	9 35	10 53	11 43	12 46	33	2 21	3 16	3 28	4 07	5 16	6 00	6 38	7 20	8 21	9 23	10 13	10 35	16
OAKWORTH	5 14	5 57	7 00	8 02	8 33	9 39	10 57	11 47	12 50	37	2 25	3 20	3 32	4 11	5 19	6 03	6 42	7 24	8 25	9 27	10 17	10 39	21
DAMEMS	—	5 58	7 03	—	8 36	—	11 00	—	12 53	—	2 28	—	—	—	5 22	—	6 45	—	8 28	9 30	10 20	10 42	23
INGROW	5 20	6 02	7 05	8 06	8 39	9 43	11 05	11 52	12 56	42	2 31	3 25	3 46	4 15	5 24	6 06	6 47	7 28	8 31	9 33	10 23	10 46	27
KEIGHLEY	5 24	6 06	7 11	8 10	8 43	9 47	11 06	11 55	1 00	45	2 35	3 29	3 40	4 24	2 25	3 06	1 26	5 27	5 28	8 35	9 36	10 49	11 30

SUNDAYS

	am	am	pm	pm	pm	pm	pm	pm
OXENHOPE	7 25	11 25	2 20	3 55	6 50	8 02	9 26
HAWORTH	7 28	11 28	2 23	3 58	6 53	8 05	9 30
OAKWORTH	7 32	11 32	2 27	4 02	6 57	8 09	9 33
DAMEMS	7 35	—	—	4 05	—	—	—
INGROW	7 37	11 37	2 32	4 09	7 03	8 15	9 38
KEIGHLEY	7 43	11 41	2 35	4 12	7 07	8 18	9 41

SKIPTON TO GRASSINGTON & THRESHFIELD

MIDLAND RAILWAY

WEEKDAYS	am	am	SO am	pm	pm	pm
SKIPTON	8 37	11 40	10 3	12 4	3 8	5 57	7 35
RYLSTONE	8 57	12 00	30	3 24	5 8	6 15	7 55
GRASSINGTON & T	9 05	12 08	38	3 40	5 06	6 23	8 03

SUNDAYS

	am	pm
SKIPTON	8 45	7 00
RYLSTONE	9 05	7 20
GRASSINGTON & T	9 13	7 28

WEEKDAYS	MO am	am	am	am	pm	pm	pm	pm	pm
GRASSINGTON & T	7 15	7 45	9 12	12 15	3 50	5 15	8 10
RYLSTONE	7 24	7 54	9 21	12 24	3 59	5 24	8 19
SKIPTON	7 41	8 14	9 38	12 41	4 16	5 42	8 36

SUNDAYS

	am	pm
GRASSINGTON & T	9 25	7 55
RYLSTONE	9 34	8 04
SKIPTON	9 52	8 21

MIDLAND TRAINS OTLEY TO ILKLEY
WEEKDAYS SUNDAYS
From OTLEY 7 19pm 8 59pm
From ILKLEY 8 45am 9 22am

LEEDS TO OTLEY AND ILKLEY

NORTH EASTERN RAILWAY

WEEKDAYS ONLY	am	am	am	am	am	am	pm	pm	pm	pm	pm	pm	pm	pm
LEEDS NEW	7 43	7 55	9 24	11 48	2 23	5 00	5 30	8 13	9 10	10 10	
HOLBECK	7 47	7 59	9 28	11 52	2 73	3 05	5 05	5 34	8 18	9 15	10 15	
HEADINGLEY	7 53	—	9 34	11 58	—	5 11	—	8 24	9 22	10 20	
HORSFORTH	8 00	—	9 41	12 05	—	5 18	—	8 31	9 30	10 30	
ARTHINGTON	8 07	8 13	8 22	9 48	12 13	—	3 25	26	—	8 38	9 36	9 42	10 36	10 48
POOL IN W DALE	8 09		8 25	9 51	12 16	—	3 25	29	—	8 41		9 45		10 51
OTLEY		3 19	7 57	12 21	49	3 25	3 65	5 48	48	9 51		10 57	
BURLEY IN W DALE		8 37	10 03	12 28	55	3 38	5 4	7 6	00	8 54		9 57		11 03
BEN RHYDDING		8 42	10 08	12 33	2 03	3 43	5 4	7 6	05	9 02		10 02		11 08
ILKLEY		8 45	10 11	12 36	2 03	3 46	5 6	08	9 02		10 05		1 11	

WEEKDAYS ONLY	am	am	am	am	am	am	am	pm	pm	pm	pm	pm	pm	pm
ILKLEY	7 25		8 17	9 00	10 45	12 50	2 16	4 00	6 15	8 25	10 05	
BEN RHYDDING	7 28		8 20	9 03	10 48	12 53	2 19	4 03	6 18	8 28	10 08	
BURLEY IN W DALE	7 33		8 25	9 08	10 53	12 59	2 24	4 08	6 23	8 33	10 13	
OTLEY	7 39		8 31	9 14	10 59	1 06	2 30	4 14	6 29	8 39	10 19	
ARTHINGTON	7 45	—	8 44	9 23	11 08	1 16	2 36	4 24	6 38	8 49	9 02	10 28	10 44
HORSFORTH		8 05	—	8 56	—	16	22	2 44	4 32	6 46		9 12		10 54
HEADINGLEY		8 05	—	8 56	—	1 22	31	—	4 38	6 52		9 17		10 59
HOLBECK		8 15	5 29	9 01	9 39	11 30	34	4 42	6 58	4 48	7 00		9 23		11 05
LEEDS NEW		8 18	8 15	8 29	9 04	9 43	11 34	41	2 58	4 48	7 04		9 27		11 09

ILKLEY TO SKIPTON

MIDLAND RAILWAY

WEEKDAYS ONLY	am	am	am	am	SO pm	pm	pm	SX pm	pm	SO pm
ILKLEY	6 00	8 09	10 53	10 44	12 52	2 10	3 45	4 40	5 27	7 05	8 18	10 32
ADDINGHAM	6 07	8 17	10 00	10 51	12 59	2 17	2 58	4 47	5 34	6 10	7 12	8 32	10 38
BOLTON ABBEY	6 13	8 24	10 07	10 57	1 06	2 24	3 04	4 53	5 41	6 17	7 26	8 48	
EMBSAY	8 32	10 16	1 15	2 33	5 41	7 26	8 48	
SKIPTON	8 38	10 21	1 20	2 40	5 57	7 31	7 31	8 55	

WEEKDAYS ONLY	am	am	am	am	am	pm	SO pm	SO pm	pm	pm	SO pm	pm	SO pm
SKIPTON	7 05	8 22	10 48	3 32	2 00	3 45	5 40	7 43	9 15
EMBSAY	7 13	8 30	10 56	41	2 08	3 53	5 50	7 51	9 23
BOLTON ABBEY	6 22	7 21	8 38	11 04	12 45	49	2 16	4 01	5 40	5 47	6 03	7 59	9 31
ADDINGHAM	6 29	7 28	8 45	11 16	12 52	56	2 24	4 08	5 47	6 05	7 19	8 06	9 38	10 50
ILKLEY	6 34	7 33	8 50	11 16	12 57	2 01	2 28	4 13	5 21	5 54	6 13	7 13	9 43	10 55

APRIL 1910

MO MONDAYS ONLY: SO SATURDAYS ONLY: SX SATURDAYS EXCEPTED: c WEDNESDAYS AND THURSDAYS ONLY

Train Services

When the Leeds & Bradford line opened in 1846, the Midland Railway provided a passenger service at hourly intervals but reduced on Sundays. Most stopped at all intermediate stations as soon as these were open.

The timetable for November 1850 shows 14 weekday departures from Leeds and Bradford at hourly intervals from 7.00 am until 1.00 pm but less regular in the afternoon and evening. The journey time varies between 30 and 45 minutes and there are six trains on Sundays. From Bradford to Skipton there are eight trains each way (three Sundays) giving very tight connections at Shipley with the Leeds to Bradford trains. The 3.15 pm from Leeds calls only at Shipley where it allows one minute to change for Skipton which is reached non-stop at 4.08. The other trains stop at most or all stations giving an average Leeds – Skipton journey time of 1 hour 20 minutes.

The North Eastern Railway began to serve Otley in February 1865 with a service of six weekday trains each way from Leeds but with no Sunday trains. However this omission was rectified from 1 August when the service was extended to Ilkley with six trains on weekdays and four on Sundays taking a minimum of one hour for the journey.

From the same date the Midland Railway introduced five trains (three on Sundays) from both Leeds and Bradford to Otley and Ilkley. The through journey times were about one hour to Ilkley and 50 minutes to Otley. The method of working seems to have been for the train from Leeds to pause at Apperley Junction to attach the coaches from Bradford and then for the combined train to work to Guiseley where the various carriages were shunted into Ilkley and Otley portions. In the reverse direction, trains arrived at Guiseley from Ilkley and Otley. After shunting they proceeded with the Bradford coaches in the rear so that these could be detached at Apperley Junction.

When the Shipley to Guiseley line was opened in 1876, the working of Ilkley and Otley trains was improved and some ran as independent trains. But the practice remained of combining some and remarshalling them at Guiseley.

On 1 August 1877, the North Eastern Railway began a service, initially of three trains each weekday, from Harrogate to Bradford via Otley, Guiseley and Shipley.

The Worth Valley branch opened in April 1867. 'Bradshaw' for October 1867 showed six trains weekdays and four on Sundays. They served all stations except that only two trains stopped on weekdays only at Damems.

A review of services shown in 'Bradshaw' for November 1880 shows the extent of developments which had then taken place. In the Aire Valley, the main emphasis is still on Leeds to Bradford and Bradford to Skipton services connecting at Shipley. The number of weekday Leeds to Bradford trains has risen to 36 with 13 on Sundays. The timetable is littered with complications and one wonders how the public or even railway staff were expected to understand it. The first train of the day is at 1.50 am from Leeds to Bradford which is the previous evening's 9.15 from St Pancras. This calls at Armley (by request), Apperley Bridge, Shipley and Manningham (by request). Then there is a 3.25 from Leeds which has mandatory calls at Apperley Bridge and Shipley but if you wanted to alight at Armley or Newlay, it would stop on informing the guard at Leeds. If you

preferred to travel to Kirkstall, Calverley & Rodley or Manningham, it would stop but only if you were travelling through from a station south of Leeds. The first stopping train was at 5.00 from Leeds. Thereafter there was a mixture of fast, semi-fast and all stations trains spread rather unevenly through the day.

The first departure from Skipton was at 2.23 am. This train contained through coaches from Inverness, Aberdeen, Dundee, Edinburgh and Glasgow. It reached Leeds at 3.05 and was through to St Pancras. The only intermediate call in the Aire Valley was at Apperley Bridge. In order to provide Bradford connections into and out of this express, a train left Bradford at 2.25 and ran to Apperley Bridge and back calling at Shipley and, by request on the return journey only, at Manningham.

During the day there are 22 trains shown between Skipton and Bradford plus a few starting at Keighley. Nearly all have connections at Shipley for Leeds. In addition there are a few through services to Leeds afforded by trains from the Settle & Carlisle and Morecambe Lines.

By 1880, the Worth Valley service had risen to eight trips each week day plus an extra on Saturday evenings and a service of five trains on a Sunday. The first departure from Oxenhope was at 6.50 am and had to be worked there empty stock. The first advertised train from Keighley was not until 7.40.

In Wharfedale, the Midland Railway was still shunting some trains at Guiseley. There were eight each weekday from Leeds four of which ran independently and four of which still got tangled up with services from Bradford. Commuters from Bradford to Ilkley by the 5.50 pm completed their journey in 28 minutes which is faster than today's timing but with stops only at Burley and Ben Rhydding. Those lucky enough to finish work an hour earlier could catch the 4.50 which arrived at Ilkley at 5.21 with stops at Shipley (when required to take up passengers from Scotland for Ben Rhydding and Ilkley), Menston, Burley, Ben Rhydding and Ilkley. How often this Shipley stop was invoked and whether local passengers used to sneak in we have no record. The 12.37 and 2.25 from Ilkley to Leeds completed their journeys in 32 minutes with stops at Burley and Guiseley. Inevitably they also stopped at Ben Rhydding, 'when required to take up for Sheffield and stations south thereof.'

On Sundays, there was no service from Leeds into Wharfedale but a train left Bradford at 8.10 am and proceeded to Ilkley then on to Otley before returning to Bradford. The exercise was repeated at 6.50 pm but Otley was served before Ilkley.

The North Eastern Railway, which did not like running trains on Sundays, managed nine return workings each weekday between Leeds and Ilkley. The 1.35 pm from Leeds and 2.30 from Ilkley completed the journey in 38 minutes by running non-stop between Holbeck and Otley. There were four trains between Bradford Market Street and Harrogate serving Shipley, Guiseley and Otley with a journey time of 50-55 minutes.

In 1908, slip coaches were introduced on two southbound expresses passing Saltaire in the early evening. The rear coach was slipped and brought to a stand in Saltaire station where a locomotive was attached to take passengers from Scotland into Bradford calling at intermediate stations by request. This facility ended during the First World War.

The level of service which had developed by 1910 can be seen from a summary of departures from Bradford Market Street. On Monday to Fridays there were 38 trains to Leeds. The Midland Railway had 21 departures for the Otley and Ilkley line whilst the North Eastern offered nine semi fast trains to Harrogate. 28 trains left Bradford for Skipton or beyond with 12 more terminating at Keighley and another two at Bingley. This gave a total of 110 passenger trains in the 24 hours between Bradford and Shipley. With parcels, freight and light engine movements, the quadruple track was fully utilised.

In July 1910, a through Grassington to Bradford commuter service was introduced by detaching a coach off the 7.45 Grassington to Skipton at Embsay Junction. This was picked up by an engine sent light from Ilkley and, after calling at Addingham, was attached to the 8.30 Ilkley to Bradford giving a 9.00 arrival. The return was at 5.10 pm via the Aire Valley. The 5.10 pm 'Bradford & Morecambe Residential Express' slipped a coach at Skipton which was conveyed by the 5.55 to Grassington & Threshfield arrive 6.23.

In 1924 the through Grassington to Bradford train was still running. Now leaving Grassington at 7.33 it stood at Ilkley from 8.21 until 8.30 giving a sporting chance of catching the 8.24 from Ilkley which stopped only at Menston and Guiseley to reach the wool capital at 8.52, 11 minutes before the through train which stopped at Ben Rhydding, Burley and Shipley. A faster service was available by the 8.03 from Grassington & Threshfield changing at Skipton onto the Morecambe & Bradford Residential arriving at 9.15.

28 years of passenger operation ended on the Grassington branch in 1930. Both Rylstone and Grassington stations were inconveniently sited and buses were able to reach all the villages direct. The line remained in use for freight and occasional excursions until 1969 when it was cut back to Swinden Lime Works.

Apart from temporary restrictions during the First World War which were restored soon afterwards, the pattern of train services established by the early part of the twentieth century remained largely unaltered until 1939.

The Second World War caused a significant reduction particularly at off peak times and, on many lines, passengers continued to be offered austerity level of service long after the cessation of hostilities.

Esholt Station closed in 1940 much to the annoyance of one commuter who arranged for a 'Telegraph & Argus' reporter to accompany him on the first day after closure and witness his pulling the communication cord as the train passed Esholt. It came to a stand at Esholt Junction with the desired publicity.

The Worth Valley branch lost its Sunday service in 1947 and Damems station closed in 1949. Baildon followed in 1953 though it continued to be served by occasional excursion trains and was temporarily reopened during the Suez crisis. It was never demolished.

'Bradshaw' for April 1957 shows the pattern of service which was by then so hopelessly inadequate to meet the onslaught of road competition. The number of Leeds to Bradford and Bradford to Skipton locals was about half the pre war level with huge gaps in the day time but an almost respectable service in the evening. Taking departures from Apperley Bridge to Leeds, these were at 6.59, 8.10, 8.38, 13.31, 16.04, 17.25, 18.25, 20.16, 21.10,

21.38 and 22.27. No trains called on Sundays. Keighley to Oxenhope departures were similar at 6.00, 6.50, 7.49, 13.15, 16.05, 16.57, 17.37, 18.27, 19.34 and 21.10. There was a better service on Saturdays including late evening but of course nothing on Sunday.

Bradford to Ilkley had sunk even further with Monday to Friday departures at 7.48, 12.38, 16.22, 17.00, 17.33, 17.53 and 22.20. The timetable shows just one train to Otley and Harrogate at 17.15 from Forster Square but this had, in fact, been withdrawn from the previous 25 February. There were just four trains between Leeds and Ilkley via Otley but the service via Guiseley had held up rather better with nine. There were five trains between Ilkley and Skipton.

Change was at hand. In 1957, there appeared an hourly Summer Sunday service between Leeds Central, Otley and Ilkley with some trains running through to Bolton Abbey. These trains were through from Castleford via the Methley Joint, hence the use of Leeds Central, but the real significance was their being worked by diesel multiple units. Over the next few summers, Bolton Abbey enjoyed Sunday services with half hourly dmu departures alternately from Bradford and Leeds via Guiseley. In 1960 Otley again experienced a seasonal Sunday service this time running from Bradford Forster Square to Harrogate and Knaresborough. It was not repeated.

A full diesel service was introduced on 5 January 1959 with hourly departures throughout the day from Leeds City to Bradford Forster Square, Bradford to Skipton, Leeds to Ilkley and Bradford to Ilkley. A few trains ran through from Ilkley to Skipton whilst three of the Leeds-Ilkley trains travelled via Otley.

The Worth Valley branch was excluded from the dmu programme and continued to be push-pull worked. On 1 September 1959 the TUCC met to hear BR's application to close the line. This was the same hearing which gave instant approval to the Holmfirth closure but it failed to reach a decision about the Keighley to Oxenhope service because of the weight of evidence raised by objectors. This may have been mild compared to recent events on the Settle & Carlisle line but Keighley Corporation did coordinate quite a strong case by the standards of those pre Beeching times.

The immediate result was a full dmu timetable with 15 Monday to Friday trains and 20 on Saturdays commencing on 13 June 1960. Despite an increase in custom, the reprieve was short lived and the last passenger train left Keighley at 11.15 pm on Saturday 30 December 1961. 43586 hauled a special to mark complete closure on 23 June 1962.

The Beeching Report of March 1963 recommended closure of all lines in Wharfedale, of local stations in Airedale and of Bradford Forster Square. A service was to be retained between Leeds, Shipley, Bingley, Keighley, Skipton and thence to Morecambe via Carnforth though the subsequent 'Castle Plan' of 1967 cast a shadow over all services in Airedale.

In the Autumn of 1963, a formal closure proposal was issued affecting all services to Ilkley and local services between Leeds, Bradford Forster Square, Keighley and Skipton. For the time being, Bradford Forster Square was to retain some express services to Leeds and dmus connecting with the Leeds – Morecambe trains at Keighley.

The TUCC hearing was held at Ilkley in May 1964. This

was an appropriate venue since the only organised opposition to the proposal came from the Ilkley commuters. Elsewhere the public response was feeble. In September 1964, the Minister of Transport and political architect of the Beeching Plan, Ernest Marples approved closure of 17 out of the 22 stations involved. He deferred a decision concerning Guiseley, Menston, Burley in Wharfedale, Ben Rhydding and Ilkley so that trains would run from Bradford and Leeds to Ilkley more or less as before. The remaining threatened stations closed on Saturday 20 March 1965 apart from Kildwick & Crosshills and Cononley which by then were the only ones with a Sunday service and so survived one more day.

From 22 March an increased dmu service operated from Leeds to Skipton with most trains calling at Shipley. They achieved this by stopping in the station twice and reversing at Bradford Junction. Later they found it easier in the Leeds – Skipton direction to proceed straight to Bingley Junction and set back into platform 1. A service of about ten trains operated between Bradford and Keighley.

Associated with the long awaited concentration of services at Leeds from 1 May 1967 was the diversion of remaining Leeds – Bradford traffic to Bradford Exchange.

Uncertainty over the future of the Ilkley services continued. In 1968, the Minister of Transport ordered that the TUCC procedure be started afresh and BR took the opportunity to include a proposal to close Bradford Forster Square.

It took until August 1972 to get a Ministerial decision but this, fortunately, was never implemented. The Leeds – Ilkley line won another reprieve but the Bradford – Keighley service was condemned. A limited service was to operate between Bradford and Ilkley via the pre 1876 route reversing at Apperley Junction. In October, Bradford Corporation stepped in with a subsidy to keep things as they were and were immediately joined by the local councils in Shipley, Bingley, Keighley, Baildon and Ilkley. This move, which was then without precedent, anticipated the 1974 local government reorganisation under which these towns were incorporated into the Metropolitan District of Bradford. The idea of having trains to Leeds but not Bradford cut across civic pride.

They also wanted to prevent the Shipley to Guiseley route being dismantled before the West Yorkshire PTE had a chance to consider its value.

The reopening of Baildon station in 1973 was a logical development. Frizinghall might have followed if the platforms had not been demolished early in 1972. The 1975/76 timetable allowed extra time for a Frizinghall stop but BR disagreed with the West Yorkshire PTE over the cost of new platforms.

1979 saw the long awaited opening of a main line platform at Shipley though Skipton to Leeds trains still had to reverse at Bradford Junction for a further year pending track and signalling alterations. The frequency of the Bradford – Keighley trains was increased threefold giving a half hourly service throughout most of the day. The West Yorkshire PTE financed Crossflatts station in 1982 and Saltaire in 1984.

The present (May 1985) timetable shows trains at a basic hourly interval from Leeds to Skipton, Leeds to Ilkley and Bradford to Ilkley but half hourly from Bradford to Keighley. Sunday services are two hourly in Summer with only a few Leeds to Skipton trains in Winter.

It is threatened that from October 1985, the Bradford to Keighley service will be reduced to hourly and most Bradford to Ilkley trains will terminate at Guiseley.

The closure of the Keighley to Oxenhope branch did not command universal support and 1 March 1962 saw the formation of the Keighley & Worth Valley Railway Preservation Society. There followed six frustrating years until 2 – 6 – 2T No. 41241 and 0 – 6 – 0T No. 30072 hauled the Reopening Special out of Keighley on 29 June 1968.

Accounts of how the Society achieved its objective and how it has developed since 1968 have been well documented elsewhere. At first trains were operated only at weekends but this spread to Summer Wednesdays in 1969 and by 1976, weekday operation had been extended to cover every day in July and August. There are four return workings on weekdays with seven on Saturdays and off peak Sundays. On Summer Sundays and Bank holidays, a 40 minute interval service is maintained throughout the afternoon with a total of 13 trains making up the timetable.

BRADFORD TO OTLEY

Patriot class 4-6-0 No. 45527 'Southport' stands at Bradford Forster Square with the 3.40 pm slow to Carlisle in 1964.
(Keith Preston)

A fleet of road vehicles operated out of Bradford Forster Square until this class of traffic was abandoned in 1981. *(J.C.W. Halliday)*

'Jubilee' 4-6-0 No. 45593 'Kolhapur' leaving Bradford Forster Square with a parcels train for Morecambe on 30 September 1967. *(P. Hutchinson)*

The approach to Bradford Forster Square in July 1984 shortly before removal of the signal box and most of the track. *(Martin Bairstow)*

'Britannia' 4-6-2 No. 70005 with its 'John Milton' name plates removed shunts Valley yard, Bradford on 13 July 1966. *(G.W. Morrison)*

3F 0-6-0 No. 43586 and Ivatt
2-6-2T No. 41273 stand outside
Manningham shed on 2 August
1961.

(D. Butterfield)

LNER 4-4-0 No. 2027 calls at
Manningham on 2 March 1946
with a Harrogate to Bradford
Forster Square service.

(G.H. Butland)

'Black 5' 4-6-0 No. 44943 heads
the 5.10 pm 'Morecambe
Residential' through
Manningham on 3 May 1963.

(D. Butterfield)

2-6-4T No. 42139 passing Manningham with the 16.31 Bradford Forster Square to Bristol Temple Meads on 11 August 1963.   *(D. Butterfield)*

Frizinghall Station looking towards Shipley on 26 February 1967.   *(D. Butterfield)*

4F 0-6-0 No. 44216 shunts Frizinghall yard on 15 May 1962.   *(D. Butterfield)*

45675 'Hardy' approaching Shipley with a Bradford to Carlisle freight on 19 June 1967.　　　　(G.W. Morrison)

An Ilkley to Bradford dmu passes a class 31, shunting in the scrap yard which occupies the former Shipley goods yard, on 25 September 1978.
(G.W. Morrison)

A Bradford to Ilkley dmu in the experimental white livery takes the Ilkley line at Guiseley Junction on 16 September 1978.   (G.W. Morrison)

The 11.33 Ilkley to Bradford leaving Baildon on 10 November 1979. Since February 1983 the line has been single and the former Bradford platform disused.   (Martin Bairstow)

Midland 1P 0-4-4T No. 1407 approaching Esholt with a Bradford Forster Square to Ilkley local on 25 September 1937.
(G.H. Butland)

Esholt Station looking towards Bradford in Midland Railway days. *(G.H. Butland)*

A Leeds – Ilkley dmu climbs past the former Apperley Bridge goods yard on its way towards Esholt Junction on 8 May 1976.
(Martin Bairstow)

Compound 4-4-0 No. 1087 negotiates Esholt Junction with a Leeds to Ilkley local on 22 August 1947.

(G.H. Butland)

The carnage at Esholt Junction on 9 June 1892. 0-6-0 No. 179 lies on its side. The offending signals stand side by side in the 'V' of the junction.

(K.V. Bramhall collection)

THE YEADON BRANCH

Yeadon Station and goods yard about 1960. The view is towards Guiseley. *(J.C.W. Halliday)*

2-4-2T No. 10634 and 0-6-0 No. 3878 await departure from Yeadon with a Blackpool excursion on 21 August 1948.
(G.H. Butland)

Rawdon Junction on 15 November 1958. The splitting distants are for the Leeds and Bradford routes at Esholt Junction. *(J.C.W. Halliday)*

An Ilkley to Leeds train leaving Guiseley on 10 November 1979. A hut stands alongside the platform extension once used for remarshalling trains.
(Martin Bairstow)

An Ilkley train restarts from Guiseley on 10 November 1979.
(Martin Bairstow)

Guiseley Station looking towards Leeds and Bradford on 28 September 1968 just before it became unstaffed.
(Stuart Baker)

An Ilkley to Bradford dmu accelerates away from Menston on 1 May 1963. *(D. Butterfield)*

The 11.06 Ilkley to Leeds calls at Menston on 10 November 1979. *(Martin Bairstow)*

2F 0-6-0 No. 3018 approaching Menston with an Ilkley to Bradford service on 21 June 1936. *(G.H. Butland)*

Milnerwood Junction looking towards Otley in 1966 shortly before the track was lifted.
(J.C.W. Halliday)

A North Eastern train does good business at Otley about 1910.
(Peter E. Baughan collection)

Otley Station books one of its last passengers on 20 March 1965. *(John Holroyd)*

A WD 2-8-0 heads a freight through Otley, travelling towards Arthington in 1961.   *(Peter E. Baughan)*

8F 2-8-0 No. 48352 is in charge of the demolition train at Otley on 23 June 1966.   *(G.W. Morrison)*

G5 0-4-4T No. 7240 approaching Otley with a Leeds to Ilkley train on 11 June 1947.
(H.C. Casserley)

Pool in Wharfedale Station looking towards Leeds on 3 January 1959.   (D. Butterfield)

The view towards Otley on 20 February 1965.
(G.C. Lewthwaite)

D49 62762 'The Fernie' and WD 2-8-0 No. 90230 approach Pool-in-Wharfedale with a train of empty tankers from the North East to Heysham.
(J.C.W. Halliday)

B1 4-6-0 No. 61353 negotiates the west to north curve at Arthington with a Summer Saturday working in July 1955.
(J.C.W. Halliday)

The Otley and Ilkley branch platforms at Arthington in 1961.

(Peter E. Baughan)

A 'Derby Lightweight' set emerging from Bramhope Tunnel with a Harrogate – Leeds Central – Bradford Exchange service in July 1955.

(P. Sunderland)

A Leeds – Otley – Ilkley train
approaching Horsforth Station
on 2 January 1959.
(J.C.W. Halliday)

4-6-0 No. 73054 entering
Headingley Station with a Leeds
– Otley – Skipton train on 8
August 1954.   (J.F. Oxley)

LNER Sentinel railcar No. 2133
'Cleveland' leaving Leeds New
for Ilkley via Otley on 1 August
1936.   (G.H. Butland)

0-4-4T No. 6404 approaching Burley Junction from Guiseley on 3 August 1945.   *(G.H. Butland)*

An Ilkley train accelerates away from Burley in Wharfedale on 26 May 1966.   *(D. Butterfield)*

The exterior of Burley in Wharfedale Station in 1966. The buildings were demolished after the station became unstaffed in 1968.   *(D. Butterfield)*

40112 leaving Burley in Wharfedale with a train from Ilkley on 19 April 1958.
                     (J.C.W. Halliday)

A 2-6-4T arrives at Ben Rhydding travelling towards Ilkley on 2 January 1959.
                     (J.C.W. Halliday)

An Ilkley to Bradford train leaving Ben Rhydding in May 1958. _(P. Sunderland)_

The distinctive entrance to Ben Rhydding Station in 1966. _(D. Butterfield)_

2P 4-4-0 No. 453 outside Ilkley
shed on 21 May 1939.
(John Hooper collection)

Ex L&Y 2-4-2T No. 50634 and
Ivatt 2-6-2T No. 41265 inside
Ilkley shed in June 1953.
(J. Davenport)

NER class U (later G5) 0-4-4T
No. 1888 stands in platform 1 at
Ilkley with a train for Leeds via
Otley.   *(D. Burrows collection)*

2-6-4T No. 42141 brings the 5 pm from Bradford Forster Square into Ilkley on 14 August 1956.

(H.C. Casserley collection)

2-6-4T No. 40178 about to leave platform 2 at Ilkley with the 1.33 pm to Bradford on 20 December 1958.

(D. Butterfield)

Ilkley Station on 7 June 1980 with a Bradford train leaving.
(Martin Bairstow)

Ilkley from the buffer stop end on 7 June 1980. Platform 3 was in regular use until 1983.
(Martin Bairstow)

Brook Street, Ilkley on 23 April 1966 before the bridge carrying the Skipton line was demolished.
(G.C. Lewthwaite)

40112 arriving at Addingham with a Bradford to Skipton local in May 1958.   *(P. Sunderland)*

46117 'Welsh Guardsman' passing Addingham with the diverted 'Thames – Clyde Express' from Glasgow to St Pancras in 1960.   *(P. Sunderland)*

A 2 car Derby built dmu leaves Bolton Abbey with a Sunday service for Leeds in the summer of 1960.
(P. Sunderland)

On 28 December 1964, Bolton Abbey lay under a thin covering of snow. The view is towards Ilkley.
(G.C. Lewthwaite)

Embsay Station looking towards Ilkley on 20 February 1965.
(G.C. Lewthwaite)

THE GRASSINGTON BRANCH

D5113 hauls a special off the Grassington branch at Embsay Junction on 16 June 1968.
(G.W. Morrison)

An excursion for Grassington passes the remains of Rylstone Station on Easter Monday 1961.
(P. Sunderland)

31226 and 31109 head south from Rylstone with a limestone train on 30 April 1979. *(G.W. Morrison)*

Standard 4-6-0 No. 75019 shunting at Swinden Lime Works on 1 June 1968. *(G.W. Morrison)*

On Easter Monday 1961, Grassington was host to two excursions both 4F hauled, from Bradford via Ilkley and from Huddersfield via Leeds and Skipton. 44041 waits in a siding for the other train to vacate the platform.

(P. Sunderland)

Standard class 4 4-6-0 No. 75011 in Grassington Station with the branch goods on 29 July 1966. *(M. Mitchell)*

Conclusion

Twenty Five years ago, the Aire Valley railway was operating at near full capacity and could not have functioned without the quadruple track sections. The withdrawal of local services in 1965, the loss of Leeds to Bradford trains in 1967 and the subsequent collapse of freight and parcels traffic have left it as little more than a quiet backwater.

When one witnesses the underpowered diesel multiple units struggling to maintain even a 25 minute schedule for the 9½ miles between Leeds and Bradford Exchange, one doubts whether BR selected the correct route for the concentration of traffic between the two cities.

The only real solution to serving Bradford by rail would have been to concentrate all services on one central station. Had the Midland Railway's 'Through Line' scheme not fallen victim of the disaster of August 1914, it would have gone some way towards solving the problem.

The one positive thing to emerge from the Beeching carnage was the improvement in direct services between Leeds, Shipley, Bingley, Keighley and Skipton. The journey times on this route are competitive and there are main line connections at Leeds. The reopening of Saltaire station has been acclaimed as a success but the new station at Crossflatts less so.

In contrast to Leeds – Skipton, the value of the Bradford – Keighley service is harder to identify. The distances are shorter and buses are very frequent. The decision to run trains half hourly between Bradford and Keighley underlines the two principal disadvantages of the PTE system-parochialism and the costing formula. It would be better to run hourly from Bradford to Skipton with stops at the three closed stations beyond Keighley and at the Airedale Hospital near Steeton. This cannot be done because the county boundary crosses the line just beyond Kildwick.

The West Yorkshire County Council is fond of telling us that once they disappear, the demise of the Ilkley line will follow. Having been lectured for years on what a drain they are on the PTE budget and being threatened with a reduction in service, Ilkley passengers may envy their fellow travellers in Harrogate and Knaresborough, outside the PTE area, who saw their service doubled in frequency in 1984.

During its first ten years of operation, the West Yorkshire PTE carried out a series of improvements which left almost every rail service better than it had been prior to the Executive being formed. Until recently, West Yorkshire had not been one of the authorities courting Government disapproval by putting most of their subsidies into progressively cheaper fares. But lately the PTE has been following a policy much closer to neighbouring South Yorkshire whereby fares are frozen long term regardless of continuing inflation, where the number of concessions are increased but where the level of service is threatened because the Executive is under pressure to contain its spending.

The proposal to terminate most Bradford – Ilkley trains at Guiseley may sound like a cost cutting exercise to those who automatically assume that a deterioration in service must reduce cost. An hourly Bradford to Guiseley service will occupy the dmu for 34 minutes out of every 60. On the present timetable a Bradford – Ilkley return journey requires 62 minutes running time and they say that they cannot do this with only one set. One unit could do a Bradford – Ilkley and a Bradford – Keighley return trip every two hours thus providing an hourly service on both lines with only two trains but they seem not to have thought of that.

Whether it needs to take 31 minutes for 13½ miles is another matter. The schedule is designed for 300 hp trains which are underpowered for the gradients on the Ilkley line. Some 2 car dmus actually have 600 or even 720 hp and are being used indiscriminately on all services around West Yorkshire. If some of these were allocated specifically to the Ilkley line the 31 minute Bradford – Ilkley journey could be reduced.

There are anxious times ahead for those who have followed and tried to influence the fortunes of the Ilkley line through the ups and downs of the last quarter century.

Some people would complain that the Keighley & Worth Valley Railway has failed to restore services for local commuters. But if there were a serious demand for a commuter service amongst Worth Valley residents, their remedy would be to join the Preservation Society where their voices could not go unheard. The reality is that because of short travelling distances, lack of major parking problems etc, patronage of a Worth Valley commuter service could be modest.

In contrast, the KWVR is running busy trains at weekends and on Summer weekdays. It is financially sound, thanks to its volunteer base. It gives rail access to an important tourist centre and generates a lot of traffic for BR at Keighley. In addition it preserves outdated methods of railway operation which have an aesthetic appeal but no place in a modernised network. It also provides a leisure activity for those who run it. With hindsight, the running of the last BR train from Keighley to Oxenhope may not have been such a disaster.

Appendices

Opening of lines

30. 6.1846	Leeds Wellington – Bradford Forster Square
16. 3.1847	Shipley – Keighley
7. 9.1847	Keighley – Skipton
9. 7.1849	Leeds Central – Arthington
1. 2.1865	Arthington – Otley
1. 8.1865	Apperley Junction – Otley – Ilkley
13. 4.1867	Keighley – Oxenhope
16. 5.1888	Ilkley – Bolton Abbey
1.10.1888	Bolton Abbey – Skipton
26. 2.1894	Rawdon Junction – Yeadon (goods only)
29. 7.1902	Embsay Junction – Grassington & Threshfield

Last day of passenger service

21. 9.1930	Skipton – Grassington & Threshfield
30.12.1961	Keighley – Oxenhope
20. 3.1965	Arthington – Burley in Wharfedale
20. 3.1965	Ilkley – Skipton

Closure to all traffic

23. 6.1962	Keighley – Oxenhope
8. 8.1964	Rawdon Junction – Yeadon
3. 7.1965	Arthington – Menston Junction/ Burley Junction
24.10.1965	Ilkley – Embsay
19.10.1968	Embsay – Embsay Junction
9. 8.1969	Swinden Lime Works – Grassington & Threshfield

miles				opened	closed	reopened
0	0	0	Leeds City	30. 6.1846	—	
¾	¾	¾	Holbeck	2. 7.1855	5. 7.1958	
		3	Headingley	9. 7.1849	—	
		5¾	Horsforth	9. 7.1849	—	
		9¼	Arthington	9. 7.1849	20. 3.1965	
		10	Pool in Wharfedale	1. 2.1865	20. 3.1965	
1¾	1¾		Armley Canal Road	Sep 1847	20. 3.1965	
3¼	3¼		Kirkstall	Jul 1846	20. 3.1965	
4	4		Kirkstall Forge	1. 7.1860	31. 7.1905	
4¾	4¾		Newlay & Horsforth	Sep 1846	20. 3.1965	
6	6		Calverley & Rodley	Jul 1846	20. 3.1965	
7¾			Apperley Bridge & Rawdon	Jul 1846	20. 3.1965	
9¾			Idle	Sep 1847	Sep 1848	
11		0	Shipley	Jul 1846	—	
		1¾	Baildon	4.12.1876	3. 1.1953	5. 1.1973
		3	Esholt	4.12.1876	26.10.1940	
	10¼	5	Guiseley	1. 8.1865	—	
	11¾	6½	Menston	1.11.1875	—	
	12	6¾	Menston Junction	Mar 1873	Mar 1877	
	12¾	9½	Otley	1. 2.1865	20. 3.1965	
	13¼	15½	Burley in Wharfedale	1. 8.1865	—	
	15½	17¾	Ben Rhydding	1. .1866	—	
	16½	18¾	Ilkley	1. 8.1865	—	
	19¼		Addingham	16. 5.1888	20. 3.1965	
	21¾		Bolton Abbey	16. 5.1888	20. 3.1965	
	25¼		Embsay	1.10.1888	20. 3.1965	
11¾			Frizinghall	1. 2.1875	20. 3.1965	
12½			Manningham	17. 2.1868	20. 3.1965	
13½			Bradford Forster Square	30. 6.1846	—	
11¾			Saltaire	May 1856	20. 3.1965	9. 4.1984
13¾			Bingley	16. 3.1847	—	
14¼			Crossflatts	17. 5.1982	—	
16¼			Thwaites	1. 6.1892	30. 6.1909	
17		0	Keighley	16. 3.1847	—	
		1¼	Ingrow	13. 4.1867	30.12.1961	29. 6.1968
		2	Damems	Sep 1867	21. 5.1949	29. 6.1968
		2¾	Oakworth	13. 4.1867	30.12.1961	29. 6.1968
		3¾	Haworth	13. 4.1867	30.12.1961	29. 6.1968
		4¾	Oxenhope	13. 4.1867	30.12.1961	29. 6.1968
20			Steeton & Silsden	Dec 1847	20. 3.1965	
21¾			Kildwick & Crosshills	Sep 1847	20. 3.1965	
23			Cononley	Dec 1847	20. 3.1965	
26	27¾	0	Skipton	7. 9.1847		
		7½	Rylstone	29. 7.1902	21. 9.1930	
		10¾	Grassington & Threshfield	29. 7.1902	21. 9.1930	

A return excursion waiting to leave Grassington on Easter Monday 1961. *(P. Sunderland)*